371.048

£7.95

Career Turnaround

Career Turnaround

How to Apply Corporate Strategy Techniques
to Your Own Career

Dr John Viney and Dr Stephanie Jones

Thorsons
An Imprint of HarperCollins*Publishers*

Thorsons
An Imprint of GraftonBooks
A Division of HarperCollins*Publishers*
77-85 Fulham Palace Road
Hammersmith, London W6 8JB

Published by Thorsons 1991
1 3 5 7 9 10 8 6 4 2

© 1991 International Business Writing Limited

Dr John Viney and Dr Stephanie Jones
assert the moral right to be
identified as the authors of this work

A CIP catalogue record for this book
is available from the British Library

ISBN 0 7225 2478 1

Typeset by Harper Phototypesetters Limited,
Northampton, England
Printed in Great Britain by
Biddles Limited
Guildford, Surrey

To Mrs Dillis Viney, and
to Dr Erling Refsum
the authors' favourite examples of
Career Turnaround!

Contents

Part Three: Case Studies

Preface

The idea for this book originally came from a suggestion from Thorsons' parent company, HarperCollins. They suggested that Dr Viney — whom they had just awarded a major executive search assignment on their own behalf — should write a book to help people make sure that they were in the running for such prized appointments. He receives over 500 unsolicited CVs each and every week, so we realized that there were indeed a lot of people out there who were eager to be headhunted. Together we tried to devise a really practical self-improvement book, based on Dr Viney's experience of helping people take the plunge into different corporate — and not so corporate — worlds.

As we worked we found that much of the advice he had to offer seemed very business-orientated in style and approach — we were using terms such as mission statement, objectives, image, presentation, SWOT (strengths, weaknesses, opportunities, threats) analysis of personal, market and company audit, market research, promotion, product development/branding, strategic planning, feedback/control — just the sort of advice recommended to *companies* seeking to turn their businesses around successfully. So, without trying to stretch the analogy too far, we decided to call this book *Career Turnaround*.

We are very grateful indeed to each of our career turnaround case studies for their time and interest, and for helping to bring our advice alive. We would also like to thank Jan Tromans, Esther Walker and Sue Keating for patiently and accurately typing literally miles of both domestic and trans-Atlantic tapes and hours of ruminating dictation. In addition, we would like to acknowledge each other's contributions — John's ideas and Stephanie's writing — and absolve each other of any glaring faults! Finally, we sincerely hope that our readers will be inspired to go for their own career turnaround: starting from now.

Dr John Viney
Dr Stephanie Jones
London, January 1991

Introduction: The Corporate/Career Comparison

This is not a book for those who are only vaguely dissatisfied with their current position or who think that by quitting and starting again elsewhere everything will then be better without much effort on their part. *Career Turnaround* is for people who are prepared to change themselves in quite a dramatic way in order to bring about a transformation in their circumstances, to break out of the old mould or well-worn rut and revitalize themselves and their careers. It's for people who are prepared to be adventurous, to take risks, who refuse to tolerate an unsatisfactory situation any longer.

It is possible to achieve a form of career turnaround within the same company, even within the same job. The goal is improvement — a break with the past and recognition from others that this has been achieved. The career turnaround may be a lasting one, or you may find that you go through more than one turnaround over the course of your working life. For if a change cannot be made within the context of your present employment, then seeking a new position in another company or organization is a positive step.

In presenting guidelines for how career turnaround can be achieved we have drawn an analogy with the corporate world, examining traditionally corporate concepts such as mission statements, SWOT analysis — SWOT standing for 'strengths, weaknesses, opportunities, threats' — those things to consider when making a change, product development and branding, developing plans and putting them into action, and feedback and quality control.

By borrowing these concepts from the business world we can use them to help those in need of a new image, a new direction, and upgraded performance — in a word, turnaround.

Company Turnarounds

There are of course several well-known examples of company turnarounds — those below have been chosen from the book *Turnaround* by Rebecca Nelson and David Clutterbuck (W.H.Allen, 1988). Each contains elements that can be applied to individual career turnarounds.

British Airways: a change of livery, image and quality to increase competitiveness; a new attention to detail

Tesco: new image, better economies of scale, more competitiveness, new hi-tech inputs and modernization all made for better service

Woolworth: new chief executive, new ownership, rationalization, modernization, new focus, acquisitions, new retail concepts, new name (Kingfisher)

Aer Lingus: strategic re-analysis of activities, identification of new opportunities, new marketing programme, cost-cutting

Even though the analogy may be somewhat limited, we believe that it is possible to make a direct comparison between company and individual turnarounds and use this knowledge to make the changes we desire for our own lives. The dynamics of turnaround rather than the actual details of how it was achieved are what is important here. The strategies by which the company turnarounds were achieved — new leadership, image and direction; increased efficiency and productivity; a more gainful approach to marketing; a system for identifying opportunities; cost-cutting, acquisitions, divestments, communications — all are applicable to individual careers.

Defining Our Terms

Corporate turnaround: A company that has experienced an 80 per cent or more drop in earnings, followed by a recovery during which it exceeds its previous performance levels.

Career turnaround: An individual working in a variety of different contexts, often within a company, public sector body or among a professional group of people, who finds it necessary to change: who feels unfulfilled and frustrated, whether in terms of money, recognition or personal achievement, or is not able to continue in their current role because of age, disability or change in circumstances; and who is able to make a substantial and lasting improvement through their own initiative.

To develop the analogy further it is possible to identify the ten key elements necessary for successful company turnaround, as quoted by Stuart Slatter of the London Business School in his book *Corporate Recovery* (Penguin, 1984), and comparing them with strategies that will work for individuals across a range of career experiences, leading to suggestions for a new and relevant approach to enhancing your personal career prospects and performance:

Company Turnaround	**Career Turnaround**
1. Objectives/Mission statement: Redefined corporate aims	Redefined career and personal objectives
New corporate image	New personal image
New corporate livery and style	New clothes, haircut, outlook
2. Product development/branding: Improved products and services *vis à vis* the market and quality control	Higher standards of work: are your skills in demand? Are you moving with the times?
3. Market Research: Improved marketing and distribution	Maximizing the use of your skills and targetting your sector
Better external communications	Spreading your reputation
4. Strategic Planning/ Implementation: Attracting additional investment	Making your employer invest more in your salary and training (or funding this yourself)
5. SWOT Analysis: organizational change, better resource management	Planning your work and time organizing your resources
6. Stronger financial control	Maximize earnings, make your money work for you
7. Debt restructuring, reducing debt/equity ratio	More sound personal finances getting out of debt
8. New Chief executive	New mentor, boss, role model
9. Making acquisitions	Acquiring new responsibilities
10. Improved corporate health	Improved personal health

All these strategies are necessary for improving how you do your present job, succeeding at another job within the same company, successfully changing companies or changing careers.

Fundamentals

The degree of crisis encountered in companies requiring turnarounds can vary from catastrophic to relatively minor, but most are still sound at their core. The same is true in individual careers. However much a career may have deteriorated and gone off-course, however frustrated and disillusioned a person becomes, he or she still retains distinct personal and professional qualities and experiences. It is vital to believe that everyone is fundamentally 'redeemable', and this includes you. Companies in distress, however much their share price has fallen, are never worth nothing. Both companies and people can be brought back from the brink.

Companies and individuals can have weaknesses that are obvious to outsiders — and in hindsight — which they choose to overlook. Similarly both have clear strengths on which to build, and these can become a starting point in effecting a turnaround. No company nor individual is ever entirely wrong.

Considering Turnaround

Companies find themselves getting into difficulties because they become out of touch with what is happening either within their own internal organization or to their own external markets. These are problems of awareness and communications. Similarly, individuals lose touch, get out-of-date, fail to have a sufficiently well-informed grip on what is happening in their company or organization and in the wider world in which they operate.

The main reasons why people consider career turnaround fall into two camps: negative and positive. On the negative side:

● discontent with existing opportunities
● feeling lost within a big organization
● unable to continue a current role because of age or disabilities
● boredom
● dislike or lack of respect for co-workers or superiors
● redundancy

While on the positive side
● ambition to be more entrepreneurial
● seeking a creative outlet
● looking for more contact with people
● wanting to make more money
● looking for a new challenge
● desire to have one's own business, to do something entirely new

Implementing Turnaround

1. Reassessment and Immediate Action: The Mission Statement

At the initial stage of turnaround there is a need for reassessment and action which may involve some painful decision-making. Just as a company chairperson may realize that half the workforce must be fired in order to have the means to plan successfully for the future, individuals may decide that it is necessary to leave their jobs or sell their cars or houses in order to embark on something completely new. At this point they need to clarify what their mission really is, and what it is that they fundamentally believe in.

2. Communication of Intent: Objectives

Just as a company must communicate its aims and plans, an individual must put across the fact that he or she has made a decision to effect a career turnaround. In corporate turnarounds it soon becomes clear who within the company is going to help achieve the turnaround and who is not. Similarly, individuals must look for allies in their working and personal lives who will help them strengthen their resolve. By this stage the objectives should be clearly defined and articulated. These may have to be adapted and slightly reformulated at a later stage, but it is important that they are laid out early in the turnaround process.

3. Exploration and Questioning: SWOT Analysis, Market Research

In undertaking a thorough exploration of the current situation, both companies and individuals must go back to basics. In terms of company turnaround, the questions that must be addressed include: What is the company doing? Is it doing it well? What should the company be doing? What does the company most need? How can the company be more competitive and profitable?

In terms of career turnaround, an individual should ask him- or herself: What am I doing? Am I doing it well? What should I be doing? What does my company need most — could I answer any of its needs? Does it no longer need what I have to offer? How can I make myself more indispensable to my company — or perhaps another organization or profession — and create more wealth, influence and satisfaction for myself?

Both companies and individuals then need to make strategic decisions for the medium and long term, changing direction towards greater corporate/personal growth and greater profitability/success. As companies make new investments, acquiring new expertise and product ranges, so individuals can develop new skills and new insights.

4.　Implementation: Product development/branding, strategic planning

At the implementation stage of a company turnaround, the company lays emphasis on the key products and services it can offer, on its unique selling points. These are heightened and weaknesses overcome by adopting specific strategies. Companies have recovered through improved customer care, innovation, investment in new technology, privatization, and specialization in high value-added market niches.

In career turnaround these tactics can also be used. Improving one's interpersonal skills (for dealing with colleagues and clients), increasing creativity and openness to new ideas (their own and those of others), investing in acquiring new skills or gaining proficiency with handling new technology, even leaving their job and setting up in their own business, or identifying a specialization field that they can pursue either on their own or within an organization — all of these are ways in which individuals can enhance their 'product'.

In achieving a successful turnaround, most companies find they must concentrate their efforts and resources on their core businesses, eliminating all peripheral operations. Individuals too must refuse to be sidetracked and must not allow their aims and goals to be diluted or their ambitions thwarted.

5.　Expansion: Feedback/Control

Once turnaround has been achieved, a company must be seen to expand. With finances under control and a new focus of activity, a company can start looking to the long term, finding opportunities to move forward faster. This feature of 'permanent revolution' must also be adopted by individuals. Once they have more control over their careers, they must look for continual improvement, and make progress quickly to make up for any stagnation of the past.

Pitfalls

Companies and individuals are subject to certain traps that may endanger their efforts at turnaround or cause them to be less than successful.

1. **Constant Crises**
   It is possible to become enamoured of crisis. Making increasingly big decisions, sweeping away the old and bringing in the new can be very exciting. The adrenalin flows, and keeps flowing. But a turnaround must create a *modus operandi* as well as a *modus vivendi*. It is not an achievement merely to lurch from crisis to crisis, although of course it is important to recognize and be able to take action in a crisis situation.

2. **No Time to Sit Back**
   The opposite of being in constant crisis is to sit back and do nothing. It is important to remember that a turnaround is not a once and for all process; a company or individual must constantly re-evaluate their progress, making fundamental, not superficial reassessments to prevent future crises, and being careful not to repeat the mistakes of the past.

3. **When and When Not to Turnaround**
   The need for a complete turnaround must not be confused with a temporary downturn in the business cycle. A lack of profitability due to external forces may be only temporary, and may be caused by events entirely outside a company's control. Such business cycles can affect the progress of individual careers too, and may not be indicative of the need for complete change. It would be a shame to throw away a promising career, thinking it was in the doldrums and lacking in prospects when it was only suffering a temporary setback.

4. **Hang on to the Best**
   In a turnaround situation it is particularly important not to 'throw out the baby with the bathwater'. In rejecting inefficient, wasteful and irrelevant aspects of a company's or individual's activities, it is important not to lose sight of fundamentally good qualities. These will always stand you in good stead. The important thing

about carrying out a personal audit is that you can identify what your best qualities are and make the most of them, as well as strengthening those which are weak.

Timing

Corporate turnarounds take at least five years; how long do career turnarounds take? The quickest would be a few months, in the case of changing from one job to settling down in another, although some can take a few years between the time a person realizes that he or she is discontented in one role and the time he or she seeks and finds real satisfaction in another. In the USA between 1967 and 1976, 9 per cent of Fortune 500 companies underwent a turnaround. For every successful turnaround company, two failed. How many individuals have attempted career turnarounds, and how many have succeeded? It is impossible to answer this question in quite the same way. The important thing is that if you are willing to make the attempt, half the battle is already won.

Key Words

Which words would you use to describe your career? If more of the terms listed under 'Needing Turnaround' apply to your situation than those under 'Achieving Turnaround', then this is the time for you to make a transformation!

Achieving Turnaround	Needing Turnaround
Dynamism	Frustration
Forging ahead	Reaching a bottleneck
Still on the way up	Experiencing anti-climax
Making your mark	No contribution
Expressing ambition	Frustrated ambition
The sky's the limit	Lack of prospects
Not accepting second best	Compromise
Creativity	Vacuousness
New direction	Conservatism
Responsibility	Lack of responsibility
Autonomy	Powerlessness
Variety	Tedium, boredom
Optimism, contentedness	Discontent

Achieving Turnaround	Needing Turnaround
Promotion, fast-tracking	Redundancy
Guidance, having role model	Lacking a mentor
Change/recovery/growth	Stagnation
Pragmatism/realism	Blissful optimism
Competitive analysis/ positioning	Isolation, laurel resting
Rational analysis	Shooting in the dark
Instinct	Formula approach
Risk	Caution, playing it safe
Facing the truth	Head in the sand
Taking opportunities/ challenges	Staying in a rut
Building on reputation	Neglecting reputation
Focusing	Losing direction
Clear direction	Uncertainty, confusion
Directing resources	Dissipating energy
Design/image/recognition	Facelessness
Distinctive	Nebulous
Luxury brand	Vulgarity
Flexibility	Rigidity
Rescue	Abandon
Information flow	Ignorance
Sympathy/sensitivity	Arrogance
Central	Peripheral
Wide understanding	Narrow obsession
Long-term financial planning	Short-term cost-cutting
Responsiveness	Ossification
Stopping the rot	Decay
Survival	Going belly-up

Part One

Career Turnaround People

It may sometimes seem that everyone around you is settled and contented with their job or profession, yet you would be surprised by the number of people who have changed their careers and lives. Sometimes they have done it more than once, and sometimes after working for many years in one field. In this chapter we will draw upon a variety of sources to describe to you the manner and direction of several different career turnarounds.

Every time you open the newspaper or turn on the TV, chances are that you will encounter someone who has achieved a career turnaround. We'll have a look at some of the people who've caught the media's attention — celebrities, politicians or otherwise extraordinary figures whose careers have not always been what they are today.

From the pages of *Business* magazine, which regularly publishes a selection of '40 under 40', we'll pinpoint three rising young stars in the world of British business — many of whom have worked internationally — who have already changed careers once and are making rapid progress in their new situation.

Two leading headhunters — one from the US and one from Britain — discuss a few of the outstanding personalities they have encountered, both as clients and as potential placements for top-level assignments, and the dramatic career swaps they've made.

This is not to suggest that career turnaround is only for the leading lights of public life and the business world; it can be achieved by anyone who is sufficiently determined and committed. To redress this balance, two UK-based international outplacement consultants have supplied us with stories of 'ordinary' people — many of whom had lost their jobs — who faced and overcame compulsory career turnaround. By way of further example we offer six cases of young people taking on top financial jobs; a group from a depressed area; and a woman who changed from a career as a full-time mum for one in law.

We then take a closer look at what it takes to make a career turnaround: are you the type?

Well-Known Faces

Obvious examples of people whose working lives have changed radically, bringing them into the public eye, include **Jimmy Saville**, the former coal miner turned disc jockey and TV show compère; **Anita Roddick**, housewife, mother and schoolteacher who founded the 'Body Shop' chain; **Jeffrey Archer**, bankrupt and disgraced politician turned successful novelist; and **Sir Peter Parker**, who's had a plethora of careers including the Chairmanship of British Rail.

Sports personalities inevitably face some form of career turnaround sooner or later, since an athlete's professional lifespan is notoriously brief. **Brendan Foster** was a middle distance runner who then took to managing the *Nike* sports footwear business; when that didn't work out he turned to providing sports commentary for TV and Radio. **Sebastian Coe** hopes to become an MP: he's been adopted and will run in Britain's next General election.

Beryl Bainbridge: actress turned writer.

Well-known as an actress, Ms Bainbridge has appeared in a number of celebrated West End productions. She then decided to try life from the other side of the footlights, writing six successful plays, including two for television. Her first play, *Tip-Toe Through the Tulips*, was published in 1976. Her next career move was to try writing novels. *The Dressmaker*, published in 1973, was turned into a film in 1989; *The Bottle Factory Outing* won *The Guardian*'s fiction award; *Sweet William* also became a film; and two of her stories became TV series: *English Journey* and *Forever England*.

Anita Brookner: professor and art historian before she began writing novels.

Brookner was reader at the Courtauld Institute of Art, and previously visiting lecturer at the University of Reading, Slade Professor of the University of Cambridge, and Fellow of New Hall, Cambridge. During and after her lecturing career she wrote a series of art history books, and then, during the 1980s, began her fiction-writing career. Her first novel, *A Start in Life*, appeared in 1981; *Hotel du Lac* (1984) won the Booker McConnell prize and was filmed for television in 1986. She also writes regularly for *The Burlington Magazine* and other periodicals.

Michael du Carel: from chartered accountancy to light opera.

A chartered accountant and partner in an important London accountancy practice, du Carel left the world of finance and has established a reputation as a popular opera singer with the D'Oyly Carte Opera Company.

Peter Mayle: quit the rat race and upped sticks to France.

Mayle gave up a promising career in advertising when in his late 30's and now lives in Provence. He has become a successful travel writer, and his book *A Year in Provence* won the Travel Writer of the Year Award in 1989.

Dr Jonathan Miller: doctor and director.

Dr Miller was a Research Fellow in the History of Medicine at University College, London before becoming associate Director of the National Theatre. He is still visiting professor in Drama at Westfield College, London. After a career in stage directing in London and New York, Miller directed films for BBC-TV, including *The Body in Question*. He then became executive director of the BBC Shakespeare series, and directed seasons at Stratford, the Barbican and the Old Vic. Formerly artistic director of the Old Vic, Miller is still Research Fellow in Neuro-psychology at the University of Sussex. He has also directed opera, including many productions for Glyndebourne, Sadlers Wells and the English National Opera. In addition to these talents he has edited a highly respected book on Sigmund Freud.

Jeffrey Tate: from medicine to music.

Tate is now principal conductor with the English National Opera, despite being severely disabled with curvature of the spine and spina bifida. He originally trained and qualified as a doctor at Cambridge and St Thomas', London respectively. At the time he felt that he wanted to be financially secure and that he owed a debt of gratitude to the medical profession, but music was his obsession. He applied to study coaching at the London Opera Centre, and was persuaded to accept the resulting offer. He was then offered jobs by a number of conductors. He was worried about his ability to manage physically, but has succeeded in proving himself beyond doubt.

In a less serious attempt at career turnaround, **Anthony Holden** gave up writing for a life of gambling. The prize-winning journalist turned writer and biographer 'set aside his status as an amateur poker player as well as what passes for a normal life to see if he could cut the mustard on the international professional poker circuit. At the close of a bizarre 12 months, capped by a second consecutive appearance in the world poker championships in Las Vegas, Holden calculated that his precise net profit as a professional poker player has amounted to $12,300 after covering all costs including crossing the Atlantic 16 times in eight months.'* This was an experimental career turnaround to provide material for Holden's book, *Big Deal: One Year as Professional Poker Player*.

Politicians have a rather precarious existence: only the minority keep their seats until retirement. Inevitably, therefore, the field of politics includes many examples of career turnarounds. Some come to politics after years in an unrelated field; others go on to pursue alternative careers after losing their seats.

Virginia Bottomley: from lecturer and social worker to MP.

First a lecturer at a further-education college (from 1971 to 1973), Bottomley then worked for nine years as a psychiatric social worker at the Maudsley Hospital's Brixton and Camberwell Child Guidance Units. In May 1984 at the age of 36 she was elected MP for Surrey South West. She has served as Parliamentary Private Secretary (PPS) to the Minister of State for Education and Science (1985-86), to the Minister for Overseas Development (1986-87), and to the Secretary of State for Foreign and Commonwealth Affairs (1987-88). Since 1988 she has been Parliamentary Under-secretary of State at the Department of the Environment.

Robert Kilroy-Silk: politician turned TV presenter.

Kilroy-Silk started his career as a lecturer in political theory at Liverpool University before his election as Labour MP for Ormskirk in 1974. He acted as PPS to the Minister of Arts, became Opposition front bench spokesman on Home Office affairs, joined the Civil Liberties Group, and became particularly concerned with penal reform. He gave up politics and has been a television presenter with the BBC since 1987. In addition to his current TV work he writes regularly for *The Police Review*, *The Times*, and *Today*.

* *Financial Times*, 8-9 September 1990.

Dr David Owen: qualified as a medical doctor before becoming an MP.

Dr Owen gained his medical degree from St Thomas' Hospital, becoming a Neurological and Psychiatric Registrar before accepting a post as a Research Fellow at St Thomas' Medical Unit. He has remained Governor of Charing Cross Hospital and has written extensively on medical matters. Originally elected as a Labour Member in 1966, Dr Owen was one of the founders of the Social Democratic Party (SDP). His political appointments have been wide-ranging, with positions at the DHSS and the Departments of Defence, Foreign and Commonwealth Affairs and Energy. His resignation as leader of the SDP over the issue of the merger with the Liberal Party has engendered widespread speculation on the subject of what his next career move will be.

Career Turnaround has become almost a standard feature of the generation that grew up in the 1960s, an era that produced many people with flexible ideas of what they wanted to do. Many are now reaching mid-career point: two in particular, just hitting 40 in 1990, have shown distinct elements of Career Turnarounds in their lives so far.

Bruce Oldfield is a classic 1960s career turnaround case. Dubbed 'Britain's most famous Barnardo's Boy', he has gone from orphanage to being a top fashion designer with none of 'the yardsticks of the old Establishment. There was a levelling off of the classes, which had its roots in the late 1960s. A working class, Northern lad like me was given a chance.'

The most well-known 1960s product is **Richard Branson**. 'It is only in the past 15 years that one has not been too embarrassed about being a reasonably successful entrepreneur. In those days it was not the done thing.' As a teenager Branson left school without qualifications and launched a student magazine, effectively running his own company at age 15. 'As a boss, I hope I am different. I believe very much in small units and in small groups of people working together; I feel that in big tower blocks they get lost in the corridors of power. We try too to go into the kinds of businesses that all staff can be proud of, not just businesses that make money. And because people are proud — say, of the artists that we sign — the end result is that it is profitable as well.'

Three from '40 under 40'

Recently *Business* magazine published a list of '40 under 40', including three examples of rising stars in the UK who have at their relatively tender ages already achieved career turnaround.

Paul Drayson: an engineer by training who is now the managing director of a food company.

In his first career Drayson worked as a production engineer at Austin Rover and BL Technology while completing a PhD on industrial robotics. He expected he would always be an engineer. It was only when he was hired by Trebor, a company best known for confectionery, to advise on exploring the business opportunities of using robotics that he discovered his financial acumen and a way to combine it with technical expertise. Convinced that there is a 'massive market for a food company that makes imaginative, wholesome foods', Drayson, 30, led a management buy out (MBO) of the Lambourne Food Company at the end of 1988. His strategy was and is to create products that are unique and difficult to copy, such as 'Scooples Crispbread', a scoop-shaped snack that Lambourne Foods launched successfully in the UK, and which Japanese supermarket buyers are considering importing (because, Drayton says, 'the Japanese can pronounce Scooples without difficulty'). Drayton continues to be surprised at the direction his career has taken.

Mark I'Anson: an academic who has proved himself as a computer entrepreneur.

I'Anson is a rare example of an academic turned successful

businessman. In 1981, along with another Open University Research Fellow and £75,000, he set up the company Integrated Microproducts (IMP) to build multi-user computer systems. Once again from humble beginnings in Consett, County Durham, IMP now has a multi-million pound turnover and a subsidiary, Parallel Computer, in California's Silicon Valley. At the closure of its steelworks Consett was desperate for new industry, and his experiences with British Steel had taught I'Anson the rudiments of business. He says BS helped him to create a business plan — 'I wasn't really aware of what one was', he admits — and encouraged him in raising backing. I'Anson owns 24 per cent of IMP and, since it bought Parallel in 1988, spends three weeks a month in California.

Sophie Mirman: typist at Marks & Spencer who became the founder of Sock Shop.

Mirman did not go to college ('M&S is the best university for management' she says). In 1981, she joined Tie Rack and quickly became Managing Director. While there she had the idea for a similar specialist shop selling tights, stockings and socks in convenient locations such as tube stations. She set up the Sock Shop in 1983 with her husband Richard Ross and a £45,000 bank loan. By 1987, it was strong enough to be launched on the US market. There are now 130 Sock Shops, with branches in the UK, US, France, Belgium, and Ireland, and an annual turnover of over £30 million. Despite the downturn in the retail market, Sock Shops profits remain relatively stable. Consumers will not tire of the concept, Mirman says. 'That's like saying someone will get sick of buying a newspaper from a newsagent.'

Sophie Mirman has since left Sock Shop and experienced a further career turnaround, working on a new concept in retailing for mothers-to-be.

Headhunters' Choice

Gerry Roche, the Chairman of Heidrick and Struggles in New York, is one of the most celebrated executive search recruiters, and has himself achieved a remarkable career turnaround, from a potentially high-powered career as a marketing executive with Mobil to the then-unknown world of headhunting. His examples of those achieving career turnaround include the following (he placed Glavin and Townley himself!):

Nick Brady: from dealing in private money to overseeing public money turnaround.

'He made a fairly radical change from heading Dillon Read, a worldwide investment banking house, to becoming US Secretary of the Treasury.'

De De Brooks: from the world of banking to the art world turnaround.

'She made quite a switch from Citicorp to the Presidency of Sotheby's North America branch.'

Bill Glavin: from a place in industry to a seat in academia turnaround.

'A fine example of someone who left the business world (he formerly ran Rank Xerox and went on to become Vice Chairman of Xerox) and is now in academia, as the President of Babson College.'

Russell Palmer: accountancy to dean of a business school turnaround.

'After many years of running Touche Ross, Russell went on to a seven-year tour as Dean of the Wharton School [the University of

Pennsylvania's prestigious business school]'.

Pete Townley: in and out of academe turnaround.

'His career includes several changes. He was an Executive Vice President at General Mills before becoming the Dean of the School of Management at the University of Minnesota. I placed him as the President of the Conference Board, a very powerful association for companies worldwide.'

Other career turnaround success stories include **Richard Schubert,** who moved from industry to the not-for-profit sector, with a transition from Bethlehem Steel to the American Red Cross; **John Raynolds,** who moved from the corporate world to head up Outward Bound USA, and claims, 'I don't make a fraction of what I used to earn, but I wouldn't trade this job now for the world'; **Bill Bradley,** now a Republican Senator for the State of New Jersey, who was formerly a professional athlete; **Ed Ney,** a former chairman of Young & Rubicam, the global advertising agency, who is presently the US Ambassador to Canada; **Shirley Temple Black,** the ex-child movie star who became the US Ambassador to the United Nations; and perhaps the most famous American example of career turnaround, **Ronald Reagan,** ex-actor and ex-President.

Dr John Viney, the joint author of this book, has spent more than ten years in the field of executive search, and now heads Heidrick and Struggles' London office. He has been instrumental in several career turnarounds, especially involving cross-cultural moves, particularly from the US to the UK and vice-versa, a policy which has become one of the hallmarks of his approach to executive search. His career turnaround examples include the following, many of whom were his placements or clients:

Mike Dawson: from the backroom to the sharp end turnaround.

'He was really the man who floated Tunstall Telecom, and he did that very well. He started off as an accountant and saw Tunstall, saw the opportunity, bought the owners out, developed the business and took it to the market. It took an unusual person to see the potential in that business, to have insight and to take some risk. As in the case of many of the career turnaround examples, one of the most important elements here is the amount of financial risk and sacrifice that many of these people have made.'

John Duerden: corporate to entrepreneurial turnaround.

'Fifty years old this year, Duerden spent 18 years with Rank Xerox, in a variety of roles in many countries of the world, until I persuaded him in 1987 to go to Reebok, where he now runs Reebok worldwide. Duerden is a good case of somebody who has come out of a giant corporation into a truly entrepreneurial footwear company. Reebok has a lot of pace, drive and energy, but it's not much of a "corporation", and he's trying to bring to them a new way of improving how the management works. Duerden was considering a change for some time. I had tried him on five or six different jobs before it clicked with Reebok; the turnaround process here was probably over a period of three or four years. I knew he could be changed into something different, but it was a case of finding out what it was. All the time I was hunting for a cultural fit for Duerden, and we found it in Reebok.'

Gene Lockhart: US to UK turnaround.

'I have brought in a number of Americans and put them into British roles, which in most cases reflects quite a dramatic career turnaround for these people. For example, Gene Lockhart had a career in the States in a computer consultancy; and he is now running the retail banking operations for Midland Bank.'

Keith McCullagh: big corporate to new start-up turnaround.

'Now CEO of British Bio-technology, which he helped to start up, McCullagh is another example of a turnaround subject who came out of a corporate background — with G.D. Searle — and went into biotechnology. He's had three careers, having been trained as a vet, and he could have just stayed being a vet. He's another example of a man with a vision who has already taken his business to the market.'

Sir Kit McMahon: public money to private money turnaround.

'McMahon started off his career as an academic at Balliol College, Oxford. He was born in Australia and came to Britain as a young man. He went to the Bank of England — where he was Deputy Governor — then he moved to private sector, becoming Chairman and Chief Executive of Midland Bank.'

Anthony Saxton: dustman to headhunter turnaround.

'He has had a very wide variety of careers, judging by an article I read about him.* He started medical school, hated it and left to join the Royal Navy. He began his commercial career at 21 as a London dustman, moving into marketing at Goya Foods. The experience he gained there took him into G-Plan Furniture, where he became international director at age 28. In 1964 he went into advertising and, after working for five agencies, joined the executive search consulting firm John Stork & Partners in 1978. In 1986, along with **Stephen Bamfylde**, he set up his own headhunting firm.'

---

* *The Independent*, 16 September 1990.

Women and Career Turnaround

Dr Viney goes on to say: 'Arguably, women are natural at career turnaround, because many have achieved it simply by going back to work after having a family. In the business world, in my experience, I would include **Linda Keen**, who ran the systems side of Willis Faber, and who's had a number of different careers. With her husband she now runs her own international consultancy very successfully. She's terribly able and enthusiastic. In the City there are a number of very tough women in personnel, such as **Kathryn Riley** at County NatWest, **Jane Kibbey** at Shearson Lehman, **Sue Cox**, formerly of Schroders and now at Abbey Life, and **Sydney Smith** at First National Bank of Chicago. Ms Smith worked for Arthur Anderson, then went across to a bank while she was in her mid-30's. Another is **Rhianon Chapman**, who used to be at the Stock Exchange, and is now wondering what she would like to do next.

From Outplacement

Drake Beam Morin, 'Consultants in the Management of Human Resources', are among the oldest-established international outplacement and career counselling firms. They serve a wide range of client companies, from major multinationals to small non-profit organizations, and work out of 80 offices worldwide, including 45 in the US. Over 95 per cent of the executives on DBM's individual outplacement programmes obtain posts equal to or better than their previous positions. For terminated employees below executive level, DBM hold outplacement group workshops.

Their client profile is 93 per cent male, with an average age of 41. The average base salary of people entering the programme is £36,977, compared with the £47,975 they earn in their new careers. Of DBM's clients 55.9 per cent improve their salaries and 34 per cent remain at the same wage; only 9.3 per cent take a cut in pay.

DBM have noticed that increasingly people are changing careers, as the days of stable employment in a big corporation are perhaps over. It now seems that the perception among corporate executives is that the corporate life is no longer completely safe. The company has also become aware of a distinct trend towards self-employment, and the kinds of jobs their clients go into on leaving the programme include consultancy (23 per cent) and franchising (2.3 per cent) — although most of their clients were not previously involved in either of these fields.

Over half of their clients come to them as the result of redundancies, 27.5 per cent as the result of mergers, and 14 per cent because of 'chemistry'. The average length of time for which severance pay is received is 8.2 months, and the average transition time between jobs is only 12.3 weeks — so most of their clients are helped to find new jobs before their redundancy pay runs out.

Nearly 60 per cent of their clients find new jobs through networking or personal contact, 18.2 per cent from advertisements, 19.8 per cent through executive search and 2.7 per cent through direct mailing.

DBM's London consultants — Peter Trigg, Sidney A. Simkin, and Ian MacPherson — suggested the following examples of career turnarounds, from among the many clients they have helped over recent years:

Allan Clarke: from the City to landscape gardening.

Clarke was with Merrill Lynch for twelve years, rising up from office boy to achieve a salary of £100,000. He then decided to pack it in on the grounds that his luck might run out at any minute. He joined a landscape gardening firm, and then bought his own business. His is an example of someone close to the top who decided he wouldn't get there, so gave up and decided to do his own thing.

David Graves: from Rolls Royce to lecturing at Sunbridge Park Management College.

Graves had worked for Rolls Royce and was then with Fisher Controls of Lewisham for five years. Even though he has no degree, he was appointed course director of Sunbridge Park while still in his mid-40s. This is a sure sign that business schools are becoming more and more interested in establishing close links with the actual business community rather than recruiting their leadership from within academia.

Bernard Gray: from Chase Manhattan to deputy editor of *Investors Chronicle*.

Gray was a Cambridge graduate who joined Morgan Grenfell and then worked for Merrill Lynch. When he lost his job, his wife, a Cambridge don, encouraged him to become the deputy editor of *Investors Chronicle*. He was interested in and took up this position although it meant a cut in salary, from £80,000 to £30,000.

Doug Prior: ex-manager with the Colgate Palmolive corporation; now runs and teaches at his own language school.

Prior, a former Colgate branch manager, has since set up a language school with his wife, preparing the brochure and doing all things necessary to get their new business off the ground.

Peter Webb: ex-RAF, now a tour operator.

Webb's tour company is a franchise operation: he has brought discipline and strong organizational skills to the business.

These and other career turnaround examples show that franchising has become a popular alternative to working in a big corporation. As part of a franchise people are given a license to trade under an established name, and in return their turnover is subject to royalties. The franchising handbook — available from DBM and other outplacement firms — explains exactly how this is done. Over half the high street businesses are now franchise operations.

Together with franchising, many people are becoming increasingly interested in setting up their own consultancy operations. In this and other career changes, many have been supported by a spouse, thereby providing a measure of financial independence. DBM consultants feel that most people can effect career turnarounds only when they have some sort of financial support. Many have been helped by redundancy money, or even assets from the sale of stocks and shares, or of their own company in a sell-out situation.

They also quote **Adam Faith** as an unusual case study: through the success of his musical career he became interested in stocks and shares. Investing the money he made as a pop star, he became more interested in stocks and shares than in his musical career. He now edits the business pages of *The Mail on Sunday*.

The concept of career turnaround, DBM agree, is arguably no longer an abstract theory but a very necessary reality. DBM point out that many people are capable of having multi-careers, especially those who thrive on change and continued learning, growth and development. DBM have found others more difficult to advise, particularly those who do not adapt easily or have any special desire to expand their horizons.

All Around You

Breaking Away from the City

Next we examine six instances of financial whiz kids moving into completely new areas — as quoted in the *Sunday Times Magazine* .* They represent the many who have become cynical about the cut-and-thrust world of the City and who are conscious of its lack of security.

Tim Roupell was a commodity broker in sugar before setting up his company, Daily Bread, in 1986. It now supplies 800 sandwiches a day to a variety of organizations within London. His customers include Mrs Thatcher: her cheque in payment for a delivery hangs framed in Roupell's office. Roupell left the City because 'when you reach your 30s and see more dynamic people in their 20s, the appeal goes. In working in commodities, you don't know how to do anything else. The idea of sandwiches came when I found it impossible to find a sandwich which was half-way decent.' Daily Bread now has a turnover of £300,000 a year, and has as yet been unaffected by the recession.

Nigel Crawley, formerly an aviation broker, now works as a muralist, creating idyllic landscapes and classical scenes on other people's walls. He had studied art but then chose to go into the City. After six well-paid years he realized that he was no longer enthusiastic about broking. Friends gave him commissions for his artwork at first, and through word of mouth he has built up a business

* *Sunday Times Magazine*, 16 September 1990.

that keeps him as busy as his work in the City used to. 'I don't long for the pressure, the requirement to have long boozy lunches or do someone else's bidding, but I do occasionally long for the salary. The plus side is quality of life, and if I drink herbal tea these days I am not considered cranky.'

Jeremy Wilkinson earned big money advising embattled companies and buying ailing businesses. He even bought a shipyard in Holland and won the contract to refit a boat — the *Trump Princess*, owned by Donald Trump. He achieved his ambition of being a managing director of an international group by the age of 32, but then decided to leave the City. He joined a health club to lose weight and decided that the clothes worn on the high-tech equipment could do with revamping. With a partner he launched Fizz, a sports and leisure wear collection. He then bought into the company Monaco Films, and is now working on a dynamic new financing scheme whereby investors put seed money into a portfolio of different films rather than into just one production. 'The City gave me a way of looking at situations, working out financing and dealing in venture capital. I think of myself as having left the City to become a man involved in the creative arts, but hearing myself talk I see how much the City is still part of my life.'

On the days when Eurobond trading was most hectic, **Maureen Jones** would look forward with relief to her after-work aromatherapy sessions. Eighteen months later she is in partnership with two other former Eurobond traders, **Karen Lesar** and **Joan Caston**, running Verde, a company that deals in essences and cosmetic products. It was a move thrust upon them: the company they were working for had a 'management reappraisal', and all three women were made redundant. They formed a partnership with **Ruby Cook**, an aromatherapist, took a variety of courses, and invested everything they had saved. 'The fear that we might have got it wrong was more frightening than anything we ever did on the trading floor'. An upward growth in sales has set in motion plans for a retail outlet for their 36 products. But rich they are not, and all acknowledge that they are on far lower salaries than they would be in the City. However, they have few regrets: in what other business can you work yourself to exhaustion and know that the cure lies in your own hands?

As a stockbroking analyst, **Mary Corran** was expected to predict how well the large oil companies such as BP and Shell would be doing in the future. She was earning £80,000 a year, but after seven years at the job felt a nagging desire to write. 'I felt I had said all I could as an analyst, and a voice inside was urging me "if you want to write you had better get on and do it" but there was no way with a job as demanding as mine that I could have written as well. I had to choose.' She made herself write a novel in two months. 'It was absolute tripe: sickening romance. I found it boring and funny in all the wrong places so I have shown it to no one. But it enabled me to develop a working habit.' She saved up enough money to live on for two years and although she has written a children's book and has almost finished a long fantasy novel her money is running out. She lives in the hope of a publisher's advance but is still happy with the choice she made.

Mark Rowse and **Dan Briggs** have replaced bonds and equities with begonias and hydrangeas. In the City, 'we both had the feeling we were giving too much time and energy to our work without having a stake in it.' They exchanged contracts for The Flower Corporation, and handed in their notices just as the stock market crashed in October 1987. They successfully rescued The Flower Corporation's business, buying direct from Holland and fitting their delivery vans with refrigerated interiors. They have not yet matched their City salaries, but now have a capital asset.

Up from the Ashes

Career turnarounds can come out of the collapse of an old industry just as much as they can be the result of the creation of a new one. The demise of British Steel in Consett, County Durham, left many hundreds out of work. Yet out of the ashes rose a particularly surprising phoenix: 200 ex-steel workers found themselves preparing garlic croutons and chili chips rather than manufacturing steel. It was all part of the creation of the startlingly successful snack business, *Phileas Fogg.** **Roger McKechnie**, who along with four other directors of Derwent Valley Foods founded this extraordinary business in 1982 on the site of industrial decay, has since become the uncrowned king of adult nibbles. At that point unemployment in the region stood at a massive 27.2 per cent. Among the few small businesses attracted by grant aid to the devastation of Consett, McKechnie appeared with a concept so frivolous it was almost insulting. They had no 'product' as such, just the conviction that there was a gap in the snack market for exotic appetizers for adults. Coming from marketing and advertising backgrounds, the founders persuaded financiers and the Consett and Derwentside Industrial Development Agency to help them create a business. The choice of

* *The Sunday Times*, June 1990.

the brand name (Phileas Fogg being the hero of Jules Verne's *Around the World in 80 Days*) was an inspired literary allusion. The company has been growing at 35 per cent a year, and has achieved a turnover of more than £10 million, proving that the workers have made a great success of their mass career turnarounds from steelmen and -women into makers of unique snacks.

Starting Over

Gillian Pearl's story is described in the 1990 *Hobson's Law Casebook*. Her case is only one of the many examples of women who have gone back to their former careers or even started new ones after a number of years of working as a homemaker and mother. Pearl was married with two children before she even thought about university or a career as a solicitor. She had been at home for several years, and was not sure she could cope with university let alone entering a law firm. But determination got her a law degree at Cambridge as well as articles at one of that city's largest firms, Hewitson, Becke and Shaw. 'The firm has been very understanding,' she says, 'and I have worked in several general areas.' She now concentrates on civil litigation.

Considering Career Turnaround

There are clearly two phases of career turnaround. Firstly there are the people who are in their late 20s and 30s who have had one career and then turn to another. Secondly there are those who in their 40s or even 50s decide to change careers. They may have had career turnaround forced upon them as a result of redundancy. Motivations will be different for each of the two phases.

Phase One

You can readily identify with what would motivate a younger person towards career turnaround: the desire to make rapid progress, or to make more money, or to do what they most want to. They are ambitious, they've got drive, energy and motivation — for them the job change is a way of grabbing their chance of fulfilment and career satisfaction.

Mentors and Influences

What underlying factors can influence a Phase One career turnaround? Firstborn children tend to be high achievers: this fact is well-documented. There is also a strong correlation between those who've had an unsettled childhood and those who achieve early success. An unsettled childhood can produce a desire for change; early disappointment can provide the impetus to correct past mistakes or the resolution not to repeat the destructive patterns of the past. Financial or other forms of security can be seen as the way to keep the future from being like the past.

A strong parent may become a role model, for better or worse. On the plus side a family tradition of motivation, strength and success can be a positive influence. But if our parents have been very successful we may want to or be forced into trying to emulate their accomplishments — this can result in an early career turnaround situation, when the realization hits home that we are not our parents and cannot relive their lives.

Then we have people with quite a lot of natural ability but little motivation. They're bright, but they're laid-back, they don't have the drive, energy or determination to succeed. For them traditional notions of winning are simply not that important. Such people see work as just one part of their lives — they have a more balanced outlook, as human beings they are more well rounded. To be a high-flyer, wanting to achieve a lot in one area of your life, you have to be prepared to sacrifice others.

Others who make an early career turnaround are often the over-achievers — they may appear cold, determined, ruthless but it's just that they are single-minded in their pursuit of personal excellence. Such people are always on the lookout for new challenges, and they will relish casting around for a new job and changing position in life.

Phase Two

Phase two career turnarounds — in an older age bracket — spring from different motivations. The career changes of a person in his or her 40s or 50s can often be influenced by relationships and their breakdown. Divorce can make people rethink their lives, particularly if they've suffered a loss of income or change in circumstances as a result. Divorce can also produce feelings of self-doubt or even inadequacy. To combat these a person may be motivated to seek career turnaround.

Another motivation may be inspired in the workplace by up-and-coming younger co-workers who seem to be advancing faster than you feel you should be. This leads necessarily to a certain amount of frustration and re-evaluation.

Going 'Ex-growth'

In other instances older people may come to feel that their job no longer has any intrinsic value; these people have gone 'ex-growth'. They've reached a certain level in their organization, and in order to go much further they would have to put in a lot more effort, effort which they are unwilling for one reason or another to make — they're comfortable where they are. These are people who say 'I've been in this corporation 20 years and we've had 20 reorganizations so I've wound up doing 11 jobs. I've done my best and I've come as far as I can, and I've reached a good level.' We have here the classic middle manager.

What would make these sorts of people actually go for career turnaround? It would have to be something quite dramatic, because at the moment they're quite contented. If they are truly 'ex-growth' they are probably not investing any more into their careers: they're not staying late at the office, not going to try harder, not going to improve, they're just going to stay there. This scenario sums up millions of people, and represents the biggest single catchment area for career turnaround.

Turnaround by Example

One factor that might influence such people is when a close friend or colleague sets the example. Perhaps she's been with the company for 20 years — suddenly she's going off with her husband to start up in the hotel business. Even closer to home, perhaps their husband or wife is making a change. If the children are now grown a wife might be going back to work, carving out her own career. This can act as a deterrent, of course, making the husband feel rather depressed if he perceives his wife as more successful than himself, or it can spur him on to greater heights. By making a change of his or her own your spouse may bring new people into your world, people with whom you can network.

Further mid-life influences — which can happen almost out of the blue — include being made an offer of an entirely different job. This could be the impetus behind a phase one turnaround, of course, but is more likely to happen to someone with proven talents, and especially if those talents are not being used to the best advantage. Maybe a friend has offered something: 'I've left this and gone into this, why don't you come and join me?

Push Factors

It can happen that a form of career turnaround can be imposed on people. Perhaps their company becomes subject to a big takeover. People can undergo a sort of new lease on life; the prospects of new opportunities or money may provide the incentive that was missing before.

The influences listed above may be regarded as pull factors: they can be avoided, forgotten or ignored, and for many people they will have no effect. More influential than these, leaving less room for choice, are *push factors*. These are things that can happen to an 'ex-growth' person that cannot be ignored. One of these is redundancy, another is relocation, where their company is leaving their area and they cannot or will not move with it.

With redundancy, the up side is that their company may provide them with a large capital sum of money. For perhaps the first time in their lives they have this amount of cash to play with. Perhaps they will pay off the mortgage, or perhaps they will take a calculated risk. So you have no more job after 24 years but you have £80,000? What are you going to do — you're still only 44, should you invest in a franchise business? Where can you turn for advice?

Sometimes your company will help you. Certain organizations have been formed to create new businesses out of redundancy, such as the way British Steel set up British Steel New Ventures in the early 1980s for ex-steel workers who might want to invest their redundancy money in different enterprises. But such ready solutions are rare. The advice of family, friends, former mentors and trusted colleagues can also be invaluable at these times.

It takes courage to want to risk a career turnaround. To take the plunge, most people need to be convinced, or influenced by some sort of trigger-mechanism or catalyst. Compared with their younger, phase one counterparts the older working person will not find it easy to attach him- or herself to a mentor. They may have had a great deal of life experience — a good 20 to 25 years of working — but it doesn't make them understand a business and how it really works. Many large corporations don't encourage wide vision and good general knowledge on the part of their employees.

Still, it's not youthfulness these candidates lack so much as flexibility of mind. Many will have a dangerously entrenched view of things. They compare any new idea with what they've got in their minds already and if it doesn't compute — if they have no basis in experience to compare it to — the idea will be rejected.

There are millions of people with this mind-set, and in the day-to-day world their biggest challenge is to come to grips with this form of stubbornness and keep it at bay. Only by staying open and responsive to change can they succeed.

Features and Qualities

Career turnaround people have gone out and done something. They may have broken out of a mould that their parents have created, or perhaps they've fulfilled their parents' expectations.

There's often something quite appealing about people who have achieved career turnaround, whether early or late in life. They've had what it takes to take the plunge; this in itself can make them interesting. Of course it's impossible to generalize about the results of the experience. The motivating factors leading up to a person's career turnaround will be linked closely to his or her individual qualities and features.

Perhaps people who make a change in their careers do it out of the feeling that they've never really been comfortable with the life they've created for themselves. They may be living a life they don't actually believe in.

Some people can have an outlook-changing experience thrust upon them. Some people will respond to this in a negative, timid way, as with the person made redundant from one corporation who takes a lower- paid job in another corporation, or a job that is as similar as possible to his or her old one. Similarly, the person who goes out and selects husband or wife number three when he or she is exactly like spouses one and two.

What qualities do we find in people who can make the most of an opportunity? In the case of older people they may be in a position where they feel they can take a risk. One often hears it said: 'I could never have done this when I was younger because I had to look after and provide for the children, but now I've got to the stage where I can take a risk and I'm going to do it.' Perhaps previously they've been frustrated by circumstance: they wanted to make the break but didn't have the financial or emotional resources.

Being a career turnaround person has much to do with your attitude to risk. Risk can come in various amounts, and will be subjective: it must be seen in the light of your own achievements, and not measured against some absolute standard.

Those unlikely to tackle a career turnaround can be said to be *risk averse*. For one person moving to a different department within the same company could be perceived as a big risk.

Some career turnaround people have been looking for a certain opportunity for some time before it suddenly comes their way. Others may have reached a sort of bottleneck in their career. They might still be young and suddenly there's nowhere to go. When there's a blockage like this they can do one of two things — they can go 'ex-growth', or they can try and challenge whatever it is that's holding them back.

Career turnaround people sometimes look to the future and see another 10 or 15 or even 20 years of working life and suddenly realize that they do not want the next 20 to be a repeat of what they've already experienced. The expression 'life begins at 40' means that when people reach this age they really should stop and evaluate their past and future, looking towards the next 20 years up to and beyond 65 and retirement. Do they want things to stay relatively static, or are they bored and desirous of change?

Many types of job have a built-in obsolescence, a mandatory end to the career at 40 or 45 or 50, such as the armed services, the police, pilots, athletes, etc. These people actually must have another career to fall back on when they have been deemed to be past their physical peak.

It can be more difficult to achieve career turnaround after a very restricted life. Many make the mistake of seeing everything in terms of their prior experience: every time they tread into something new they just take their old baggage with them. People should try to realize that each new experience is precisely that; they can learn new tricks no matter how old, and anyone can achieve career turnaround.

Take, for example, two people in their mid-40s, both of whom have become executive search consultants after completely different careers. Again we come up against the issue of flexibility. One is optimistic, adaptive, and resilient: she recognizes headhunting as being totally new compared with the career she was in previously. She's started over from scratch, learning her new craft. At times she had to take a back seat and listen to and learn from others sometimes younger than herself. That's pretty hard if you've been a managing director of a business.

The second person is less successful. He lacks this flexibility. He is unwilling to accept advice from those younger than himself and refuses to accept that his old skills are not always applicable to his new endeavour.

Achieving career turnaround has everything to do with mindset. Rigidity of mind breeds stagnation, adaptiveness is the tool you need to succeed. Successful career turnaround people can 'translate' their skills, adjusting them to fit their new circumstances and not being afraid to abandon them if necessary. They can appraise their skills and see how they can be used for a whole variety of applications. Others will look at their skills and see them only as limits to how far they can go. It all depends on your point of view.

Part Two

Career Change/ Corporate Change

Mission Statement

What is your general philosophy of life?

What is your general philosophy of work?

These may be very difficult questions to answer, but if you haven't got a sense of what matters to you, you are not going to be very effective career-wise, and will certainly not be able to achieve career turnaround.

You may find it helps you to define and explain your mission statement by considering the corporate mission statements of successful companies and comparing them to your own philosophy of life and work. The mission statements of eight companies — British, Continental European, American and Japanese — have been extracted from corporate brochures and reports and accounts, and are reproduced below. Each represents an entirely different corporate culture and approach, and you will see the many similarities these have with individual traits such as personality, style and cultural background.

It may be a simple case of the words used in these mission statements inspiring you towards what you feel are worthy qualities and goals. Ideally, imagine that you are a company — you have a history, experience in certain activities, skills, achievements, a reputation and an outlook and goals for the future. Try writing your own mission statement, one that could preface your own personal 'brochure' or 'report and accounts', forming an introduction to an appraisal of your performance and prospects.

'We will continue to build business in all our main markets, whilst we are fully aware of the need to temper the pursuit of our long-term aims with particular care and prudence . . .the strength, balance and thrust of our business continues to provide solid foundations in changeable conditions. Only by planning, building and continuously adapting to changes in our industry and the economies in which we operate can we aspire to achieve the results which will provide our shareholders and personnel with appropriate long-term returns and rewards.'

S.G. Warburg Group plc

'Tesco is committed to expansion and believes the best way to secure a healthy and growing share of the market is to be innovative and efficient both in the creation of high-quality products and in the way they are produced, distributed and sold . . .The stores Tesco is building today respond to market changes and to increasingly sophisticated customer demands . . .'

Tesco plc

'Inchcape, the international services and marketing group, operates in more than 60 countries, acting for internationally-known manufacturers' products and technologies and providing skilled specialist services worldwide . . .it is the strategy of the Group to be amongst the leading companies in all our main business streams by developing these operations to meet the increasing needs of our principals as well as providing outstanding services to our customers . . .'

Inchcape plc

' "A talent for television" . . .is the key to the past and future success of this company . . .an exemplary history of service in regional programming; over 21 years as the largest commercial producer of networked programmes; and an international producer and distributor of distinction. The record reveals that Thames is "a natural" in the television sphere. It has a full range of talents that goes hand in hand with the one constant factor amidst all the uncertainties: a resolve to remain a London-based broadcaster and producer of world-class television.'

Thames Television plc

'Executive search is our profession. The search to find outstanding executives for our clients; in whichever industry or sector they operate, and wherever they may be based. This has been our profession for more than 35 years. At first throughout North America, and now across Europe and the Pacific Basin, we are dedicated to excellence and success in our consulting work. Our fundamental commitment in every assignment we undertake is: 'To identify and attract executives of the highest possible calibre who will enhance the value of our clients' business.'

Heidrick and Struggles International Inc.

'Goldman Sachs is a leading, full-service international investment banking and securities firm serving corporations, institutions, governments, and individuals worldwide. Founded in 1869, we are one of the oldest, largest and most strongly capitalized firms in our industry and the only private partnership among the major Wall Street organizations, with 128 partners . . .We steadfastly maintain the shared values that account for our past accomplishments: namely, that in supporting our clients' interests we display the hard work, creativity, collective enthusiasm and co-operation, professional standards, and respect and appreciation for each individual that gives our firm its special character . . .'

Goldman Sachs

'At the dawn of the 1990s, we believe that positive political and economic trends now sweeping the globe place us on the threshold of what may be the most promising decade of the 20th century. Success will depend on our ability to effectively manage the risks and opportunities presented by a complex, ever-changing environment . . .At Merrill Lynch, we are making choices for the decade ahead: refocussing our resources on the areas of greatest potential return, and becoming leaner, more cost efficient, and more competitive in order to meet the challenges ahead . . .'

Merrill Lynch

'Today, Japan is making great strides toward societal maturity. Japan's industrial structure has undergone significant changes due to innovative technological developments; information-consciousness now permeates all aspects of society and business. In the midst of the social and economic upheaval, peoples' aspirations and expectations have also altered greatly. In response to these changes, the Saison

Group is inaugurating imaginative policies and expanding its activities to infuse more depth and breadth into its services. The Saison Group differs greatly from other groups. The Group's activities touch, directly or indirectly, all facets of peoples' lives. The diversity of our activities enables us to respond quickly to societal changes . . .our goal is to generate synergistic effects within the Group's various operations . . .including department stores, superstores, convenience stores, restaurants, insurance companies, gas stations, food processing plants and other enterprises . . .'

Saison Group

'Our emblem is the pictogram of a mountain — a traditional Japanese symbol of the finance business — accompanied by a character taken from the name of our founder, Tokushichi Nomura, set against the blazon of the House of Nomura, a cluster of ivy leaves. In the course of our history, in which we have climbed many mountains, we have always looked beyond to the next: at the highest peaks, beyond the city of our birth, Osaka, and beyond our own country. From each summit, we have been able to look back, too, and draw confidence and inspiration from the continuity of our aims and philosophy . . .Nomura has never played a passive role. By taking an innovative lead so often in so many spheres of the securities industry in Japan, we can justly claim to have made an important contribution to the development of the country's capital markets and of its economy . . .'

Nomura Securities

Key Words and Phrases

Qualities:

- strength
- soundness
- balance
- thrust
- creditworthiness
- solid foundations in changeable conditions
- innovation and efficiency
- management and financial resources to build on progress
- experienced yet still enthusiastic

- talented, with a speciality that's the key to future success
- hard working, creative and co-operative
- professional, with respect and appreciation for others
- able to manage risks and opportunities
- information-conscious
- truly international

Experiences:
- a history stretching back many years
- activities that spread far beyond national borders
- reputation for professionalism
- climbing many mountains, but always looking beyond to the next
- a confidence and inspiration that comes from the consistency of goals and philosophy
- innovative in many spheres of activity
- never a passive role
- an important contributor

Aims:
- build business
- temper the pursuit of long-term aims with care and prudence
- plan, develop and continuously adapt to change
- aim to provide outstanding service
- be dedicated to excellence and success
- enhance the value of work for others
- steadfastly maintain values
- refocus resources on the areas of greatest potential return
- become leaner, more cost efficient, more competitive
- inaugurate imaginative policies and expand activities
- try to infuse more depth and breadth into activities
- respond quickly to social changes

Now, after considering your strongest qualities, experiences and aims in your life and in work, write your own mission statement. Include in it what you feel is important to you in both personal and career terms, what your wildest dreams are, what you see as your purpose in life. Be as vague and philosophical as you like, but do spend some time thinking seriously about this. It will form an overall background for the next step: defining your objectives.

Objectives

What are your

- — general
- — specific

goals in relation to your career, in improving what you already have, and in achieving career turnaround?

What do you hope to have achieved after

- — three months?
- — six months?
- — one year?
- — five years?
- — ten years?

What are your personal goals, in terms of building up your skills and experiences and improving your appearance?

What are your financial goals: are you aiming to maintain the status quo, pay off your debts, be able to afford a second home or car, be able to take a year off, or be completely financially independent?

What are your family goals: seeing more of them, being able to afford private education, being able to afford a nanny so that you (or your spouse) can return to work; or, if you have been raising a family, being able to make the break from the home to enter a career-track again?

The task of setting goals is crucial. It doesn't matter if they have to be revised; it would be unusual if they were not. These objectives should be referred to constantly during the entire career turnaround process.

For our 'Mission Statement' we looked at the qualities, experiences and aims included in a variety of corporate mission statements which could then be used to outline your own personal mission statement. Many of these can be developed more specifically and seen as 'Objectives'. They include:

1. Building
   establishing yourself in your chosen career
   being more ambitious
   devising a strategy to be among the leaders in what you do
   developing what you are already doing so that you do it as well
   as you possibly can.

2. Developing
   instituting imaginative policies
   expanding your activities
   trying to diversify what it is that you do

3. Adapting
   responding to market changes in your area of work
   reacting quickly to social changes
   keeping up to date in your field and your interests

4. Improving efficiency
   cutting costs
   becoming more competitive
   organizing your time

5. Improving quality
   striving to provide outstanding service
   trying always to contribute to the wider economy

6. Internationalizing
   seeing 'the big picture' and your place in it
   having a more international and less parochial outlook

7. Increasing rewards
   concentrating on those aspects of your work and home life that
   you get the most pleasure out of
   focussing and directing your efforts on established goals

seeking long-term returns and rewards
having a commitment to further growth

These seven goals encompass the themes behind what some of your main objectives could be.

Make a list of your own particular, specific goals, to be achieved before a certain space of time. They must not be so easy that there is no challenge; similarly, they must not be so difficult that you have no hope of meeting them. At the end of the time period which you are allowing yourself, you must ask yourself if you have really achieved career turnaround, as defined by you. Sample objectives charts appear below, as do blank charts for you to work with.

Objectives: Your Individual Goal Chart
Working Life   3 mths; 6 mths; 1 yr; 5 yrs; 10 yrs

1. Building
2. Developing
3. Adapting
4. Improving efficiency
5. Improving quality
6. Internationalizing
7. Increasing rewards

Objectives: Your Individual Goal Chart
Personal life   3 mths; 6 mths; 1 yr; 5 yrs; 10 yrs

1. Building
2. Developing
3. Adapting
4. Improving efficiency
5. Improving quality
6. Internationalizing
7. Increasing rewards

Sample Objectives: *Working Life*

1. Building: being made head of your department, getting promoted
2. Developing: taking on new responsibilities
3. Adapting: learning to be more computer-literate
4. Improving efficiency: buying a computer
5. Improving quality: paying more attention to detail, being less lax
6. Internationalizing: learning a new language
7. Increasing rewards: taking on outside work for more money

Sample Objectives: *Personal Life*

1. Building: being made head of your sports club
2. Developing: taking on a new hobby
3. Adapting: joining in with children's activities
4. Improving efficiency: re-organizing household chores
5. Improving quality: seeking out the best for your family
6. Internationalizing: going on holiday to a country you've never visited before.
7. Increasing rewards: treating yourself — going swimming more often, getting out more.

Write your own charts under these seven headings according to the time-frames suggested above.

To develop these objectives further, and decide which goals are most appropriate for you, it is necessary to consider your own personal SWOT (Strengths, Weaknesses, Opportunities, Threats) analysis: a personal, market and company audit.

SWOT Analysis: Personal Audit

- What are your strengths and weaknesses, skills and experiences?
- What have you got to offer? In particular, what have you got to offer that others have not?
- How do you go about seeking objective advice and opinions?
- What have you achieved so far?
- Are you happy with the position you have gained?
- What specifically could you do better?

In analysing your personal audit we will look at:

- Self-image
- Self-analysis
- Psychometric testing
- Personality types

Implementing the strategy of career turnaround can be achieved single-handedly, but the practical advice of outsiders can make all the difference. Executive search or outplacement consultants can come in and provide the vital details about how to transform a career dream into reality. They can help answer those questions of how to make others feel good in your presence; how to make them want to help you; how to network, get references, and market yourself; and how to polish up the impression you make. One way of signalling the implementation of a career turnaround is to adopt a different image.

Self-Image

To start we'll look at personal image and appearance. This is important, and not just a matter of getting a new haircut or a new suit. Changing your image is more to do with really changing yourself, from the inside, and then reflecting that new you on the outside. If everyone's always seen you as a cautious and not particularly stylish dresser, how are you going to cope with that? Is that you, and is that what you want to be?

You know the suits you've got are the suits people were wearing 15 years ago: you've got to get more up to date. Of course you wouldn't want to try to look a trendy 22-year-old, but you should at least dress for what you want to become. You've got to decide where it is you're going and how you want to look, and to think in terms of the signals you put out to people.

In implementing your career turnaround, you've got to re-evaluate everything about your life. Besides just changing your clothes, you may want to do a lot of things — get your nails manicured, modernize your taste in shoes, get a new hairstyle, toupee, rinse, or different glasses. You might want to lose or gain some weight to fit your new self: whatever it takes to look like what you want to become. If in spite of trying you're still a bit plump, wear double-breasted suits — they'll make you look better. Get a decent tailor so you look comfortable in what you're wearing. Think positively: imagine yourself in your new role and give yourself confidence.

Take the advice of good people, someone you trust, whose judgment is sound. This will in turn teach you about your own good judgment: are you able to discriminate between good and bad advice? Do you know whose advice to take?

Self-Analysis

The initial contemplation of career turnaround means re-examining career issues, and questioning the validity of your own personal recipe: what you are made of, and how you are put together? Above all, is there a potential for change? You've really got to take a long hard look at yourself.

Many people have achieved career turnaround without self-analysis, but you should take this opportunity to analyse your personality type and your strengths and weaknesses, taking stock of your situation: where would your experience be best put to use?

Your First Career

It is very important to try and delineate what you are good at, because there's a very real possibility that as a result of bad careers advice or personal circumstances you may have gone into a field that you are not particularly good at, almost by accident and certainly not in a well thought out way.

Early career mistakes happen all the time, leaving many people feeling that although they're still quite young, they've failed — that already, before they've hardly tried, they've missed their chance to fulfil their destiny. A first job is so important — but for a variety of reasons, none of which have to do with yourself, you could get the 'wrong' first job and ruin the rest of your career.

One early career problem centres around your co-workers: perhaps you're working with people you don't actually like, people who do nothing to inspire or encourage you. A lack of confidence on your part may result in your putting up with this situation rather than doing anything about it.

Social Pressures

The need for social status, either imposed by others or self-imposed, can be a big influence behind many early career decisions, often forcing round pegs into square holes. Many people think that a job in an apparently socially sophisticated environment can make up for a former lack of social status.

Pressure to go for such a career can come from peers, or parents; or perhaps you marry someone who is presumably from a different social class? This is a classic scenario — working class marries middle class — and is thereby led to try and prove itself. The composer Elgar, for example, married above his social rank and outside his religion. He had to overcome a lot of prejudice about who he was and what he did, and never the less succeeded in spite of it.

Lack of Opportunity?

Many people feel they have ended up in the wrong career as a result of not being offered opportunities. This is more often a case of failure to identify opportunities, or of being unreceptive to them. It is often up to you to make opportunities, since very often much of this perceived lack of opportunity can be of your own making, masking a scarcity of drive and determination.

Some people move in very small circles, unaware of the scope of available opportunities. This perception can change, however. A change in circumstance, such as moving house or making new friends, can increase the range of possibilities.

On the other hand, many potential career turnaround people may be good at recognizing opportunities but then lose the chance of making progress when an outsider (such as an executive search or outplacement consultant) deems them unfit to meet the challenge.

The consultant's job is often far from easy. Some people give a poor impression of their motivations, appearing dull and unimaginative. It then requires some investigation to ascertain whether they could cope with opportunity. Someone apparently unexciting on the outside could actually be quite driven on the inside. The important thing is to help people recognize your worth, otherwise you may be written off.

The job of the headhunters and outplacement consultants is to see the value in people and help them achieve success by finding them a position in which they will be happy and prosperous. But they are not psychic, and they see a great many people and can usually spend only a short period of time with each one.

The confidence factor is very important, and somebody who does not feel he or she has been particularly successful is bound to be lacking in confidence. But once career turnaround has been put in motion, your confidence will increase and be constantly reinforced by your progress.

Personality

Some types of people will never be able to contemplate career turnaround until it is forced upon them, say by redundancy. Others are spurred on by a need for heightened self-esteem, or a desire to prove themselves. Then there are people who are held back by a lack of confidence: they believe that they lack social skills, but really all they need is practice and more self-assurance.

When analysing yourself in preparation for a career turnaround, and considering whether or not you are 'turnaround material', you must take inventory of your particular strengths and weaknesses. If you don't relate to any of the items on this internal checklist, if you're not really committed to trying to build on the strengths and eliminate the weaknesses, you're probably not going to be very successful in achieving your turnaround. Below are sample lists — see which of these factors are relevant to your life and experience.

You need to take time to analyse yourself. One good way of doing this is to undergo a psychometric test. You will be amazed at what it reveals and, in a more practical way, how it will illuminate your strengths and weaknesses.

Strengths	Weaknesses
Sensitivity	Indiscretion
Independence	Acquiescence
Risk-taking	Anxious
Personal flair	Timidity
Skill at languages	Ethnocentrism
Ability to delegate	Indecisiveness
Readiness to listen to others	Arrogance
Good public speaker	Inarticulate
Careful, conscientious	Slapdash
Experienced	Novice
Willing to learn	Stubborn

Psychometric Testing

More and more people entering new companies or taking on new responsibilities within the same company, as well as trainees coming onto new schemes, will find themselves subject to a form of *psychometric testing*. It can be simple and speedy or long and involved. What is the rationale behind it, what is it supposed to reveal, and what format can you expect? One thing is certain: after a really thorough psychometric test, you will never again look at yourself in quite the same way!

Background

The concept of psychological testing has always captured the public imagination, as demonstrated by the plethora of quizzes and participatory psychological profiles featured in popular magazines. For the last decade, more sophisticated versions of these tests have played an increasingly serious role in the workplace, being used by employers for both analysing existing executives and recruiting new staff.

More and more companies are turning to psychometric testing of applicants. This is largely for two reasons: firstly, in an effort to weed out inappropriate candidates in a more objective manner than by the interview process; and secondly, to reduce staff turnover and increase human resource efficiency. This kind of testing is seen as a more accurate way of fitting the right person to the right position. Psychological testing is finding a place in the decision-making process that lies behind awarding promotions, corporate restructuring, and helping employees better to understand and represent the company's image.

Testing in Action

As companies grow larger and more diverse it becomes increasingly important for them to adopt uniform standards; in this way a company can maximize the use of its human resources and give a consistent image to the outside world. Psychological assessment offers the twin advantages of objectivity and consistency in hiring and promotion practices.

Korn/Ferry, one of the 'big four' international executive search firms with an office in the UK — the others being Russell Reynolds, Heidrick and Struggles, and Spencer Stuart — has become a leader in the application of psychological testing in the workplace, through the services offered by its recent acquisition, Pintab Associates, managed by Miss Olya Khaleelee.

Most other search firms are yet to provide in-house psychometric testing facilities, instead reluctantly engaging the services of freelancers of uncertain quality on behalf of their clients, or leaving this task solely to their clients. More and more search and selection firms, however, are seeking to diversify their services, hoping in this way to keep clients loyal and maintain business turnover and margins. Psychological testing is an ideal value-added service, and it does not conflict with other recruitment services.

A Holistic New Approach

The idea of being able to determine a person's character by asking a few questions and consulting a standard table is rightly met with great scepticism, but Pintab's product is quite different: its assessment service provides not a collection of data, but an insightful analysis presented in useful, readily comprehensible terms. By combining five recognized and respected tests with extensive interviewing and interaction with a trained psychologist, and taking a qualitative rather than quantitative approach, Korn/Ferry can ably assist in screening new recruits, identifying employees for the fast track, and deciding on promotions.

As a result of its psychodynamic approach, Pintab's service can also predict a) the performance of professional groups, b) staff turnover, and c) management development requirements. Understanding people in the round can also point to how they should be integrated with their work environment, revealing their attitude to authority and what sort of boss they will get on with, and how their abilities can best be cultivated.

The Purpose and Value of Testing

The assessment process employed by Pintab — which takes six hours in full — explores how people deal with threats, and can reveal a hidden tendency to over-react, or be prickly, in a way that the ordinary interview process could never match. This test can uncover a lack of confidence, identify whether people work better in groups or alone, and determine whether they will use an organization for their own ends or really work for it.

Rather than classifying people as types, Pintab's assessment illuminates the vital details of the *individual*. Senior managers in a good company have to think on their feet and act fast. How well do these particular candidates for promotion maintain an accurate image of reality despite being given only partial information? How well do they integrate their intuition and intellect? In a moment of crisis will they be able to act on their instincts, or will they freeze in the face of too many conflicting thoughts? This assessment package can point to many of the answers. Are these potential job candidates resilient and thick-skinned, or sensitive and easily hurt? What kind of defence mechanisms do they use to deal with aggression or stressful situations? Do they use active denial or selective inattention? In the instance of a money-markets trader, for example (a sector of the business world that Pintab targets as particularly relevant) has he or she got the necessary instinct — and confidence — to know when to sell, buy or hold?

Picking Out the Fast-trackers

Together with the growing consciousness of career development comes the need to identify the fast-trackers, that is, those deemed worth the extra investment of time and money needed to develop to their highest level of ability. With this it becomes necessary to reveal potential problems as early as possible. Undesirable characteristics can lie buried beneath the surface, revealing themselves only in crisis situations or over periods of prolonged stress . . .or under certain test conditions.

The Origins of the Tests

These tests originate in Sweden, Switzerland and the US, and are called the *Defence Mechanism Test* (DMT-Sweden), the *Colour Test*, the *Watson-Glaser* test (US), and the *Ravens* test. Of these, the DMT is perhaps most interesting.

Developed by Professor U. Kragh at Lund University, according to the theory of *percept-genetics*, the proving ground of the Defence Mechanism Test was in the selection of trainees to become fighter pilots in the Swedish air force. There had been a high failure rate among these pilots in the past, due in part to their inability to perceive obvious problems and act on them in time. Testing with percept-genetics in the Defence Mechanism Test reduced the failure rate to virtually zero.

The Defence Mechanism Test has also been used to assess a group of 257 Swedish football players, with the results of this research currently being written up in Sweden. The indications are that the Defence Mechanism Test is an excellent predictor of success among sportspeople.

Psychometric or Psychodynamic?

The image of serious psychology has suffered from the craze for pop-psychology and magazine-type quizzes, and even the well-informed sceptic could be forgiven for doubting that the ineffable character of the individual can be laid bare by scientific analysis. Admittedly, a number of the so-called serious tests currently in circulation in the business community are of dubious value. In the first it is essential to look at the difference between two types of testing, 'psychometric' and 'psychodynamic'.

In psychometric testing, a standard population profile is taken of a number of 'normal' individuals, as defined by the test standards. The results of an individual's test are then compared quantitatively against this sample, and conclusions drawn from the results of this comparison.

Psychodynamic testing, on the other hand, is qualitative rather than quantitative. In other words, the emphasis is on how the person reacts rather than on how much he scores on the various scales. Using a combination of the two types compensates somewhat for the deficiencies of strictly psychometric testing, and when further enhanced with a lengthy interview session incorporating considerable non-test interaction, a more credible and valuable result is achieved.

Six Hours of Analysis

Pintab's complete assessment lasts six hours, including a period spent discussing the results and reaction to the test in general. There are five basic tests, of which three will be familiar to many interested in this field. The two most well-known are the Ravens Test and the Watson Glaser test. The former uses a set of progressively more difficult matrices to test visual problem-solving ability. The Watson Glaser Test works in basically the same way for verbal problems, measuring an applicant's ability to think logically, solve problems, make inferences, evaluate information and draw conclusions.

The DMT: A Look into Yourself

In the DMT, the person undergoing the test is subjected to a quite strange experience, which can be both frustrating and illuminating at the same time. The individual looks into a metal box (almost like a seaside funfair peepshow) which blocks out all light except the picture it projects, flashing at the viewer.

He or she is shown a slide very briefly — for only a fraction of a second — and is asked to report on and draw what has been seen. In front of the individual is a large sheet of paper with 20 empty squares, to be filled in with drawings of what has been seen. The way the individual reacts to the pictures is revealed in the process of reporting and the drawings in the squares.

The advantage of DMT is that it is not a self-report test in the sense that the applicant has control over his or her responses. Thus it can reveal hidden traits. The pictures are designed to include nine points of recognition, the number recognized, recorded as a blip on the final scoring sheet, are used quantifiably to show the results, which can then be matched with an analysis of the candidate's emotional development.

The DMT provides a set of hypotheses about each subject, clearly indicating people who have had early responsibility, who've grown up before they've had to, and who have been fostered by a strong mentor. It can show isolation, fear of getting close to others, and the way that anxiety and fear are controlled. An individual's perception can be coloured by optimism or pessimism, activity or passivity, sameness or individuality, disregard or fear of authority, certainty or confusion in outlook, confidence or trepidation — and all these can be indicated by his or her responses to the DMT.

Above all, the DMT — as a psychoanalytic rather than psychometric test, based on one-to-one evaluation — is significant in terms of registering a person's defence mechanism, speed of reaction, and sensitivity/insensitivity. In spite of only partial information, can the subject hold on to reality? Senior people with a great deal of responsibility need to be able to think on their feet, act quickly, and exhibit resilience and tenacity. Will the person continue to be a good middle manager, or could he or she go higher, showing real responsibility and creativity?

When top CEOs are undergoing the DMT, their defence mechanisms are clearly revealed; they may be overtaking others, but not so much so that they can only work on their own. They may have strong technical dispositions, but not so much that they cannot work with others. They may see themselves as tough and assertive or benign and supportive. They may see authority as threatening or sympathetic. These qualities cannot usually be measured in a standard interview situation, nor can predictions of future performance otherwise be made.

The Colour Test: Not Just Black and White

The Colour Test also provides a glimpse below the surface. The subject is asked to arrange a number of coloured tiles — in a total of 14 shades — according to a few simple rules. The tiles are used to construct two pyramids.

The resulting pattern can then be interpreted as a key to the subject's emotional makeup, revealing aspects such as a tendency towards personal frustration or towards being over-intellectual, i.e.: the preponderance of one aspect of someone's character. The Colour Test can also delineate creativity and one's attitude towards structure and control.

Viability

The ability of these individual tests to sum up someone's entire personality might be questioned, but it is certain that they fulfil the purpose for which they are most often used: developing hypotheses to be used as a starting point for a more thorough discussion, and to provide windows to look more deeply into a person than the formal interview situation can allow. As more and more employers, headhunters and recruitment consultants use forms of psychometric testing to improve the accuracy, objectivity, reliability and consistency of their selection and assessment techniques, there will come a time when people who have *not* been subjected to at least one form of assessment will be very rare indeed. And with this development will come more converts to the value of psychodynamic assessment, because very few people who have undergone the experience remain unconvinced of its value.

Personality Types

This is a very simplified introduction to some of the different personality types that you will want to understand in order to advance your career. In achieving career turnaround you are going to come into contact with each of these types and combinations of them: you must be ready to deal with them, get the best out of them, make them want to help you, and above all, never irritate them!

Using some very basic psychology, there are four different personality types. Should you find this introductory discussion interesting and would like to know more about the subject, you should explore more detailed psychology tests, such as the Myers Briggs test.

The four basic types are: the *driver*, the *analytical*, the *expressive*, and the *amiable*. While most people are a mixture of two or more types, one type will never the less predominate. These personality types can also be related to corporate cultures and used to analyse what sort of company you might be working for now and what sort you might like to work for in the future. Certain types of people will predominate in certain corporate structures. Which type do you think you would work with best?

The Driver

The driver is tough, highly focussed and strongly dominant. He or she has little time for other issues, is fairly one-dimensional, and often likes people of the same character.

Drivers have no time for chit-chat, but get straight to the point, making their points clearly and briskly in short, hard sentences put across with a good deal of force and drive. Drivers say what they have to say and then get up and leave the room. Drivers are very business-like, professional, authoritative, and action-orientated.

The Analytical

The analytical type needs to see structure above all else, and shows great attention to detail. Analyticals like an environment that they can control — one with few unknowns. The analytical type needs to have a logical approach to a meeting, and gets worried if deviations occur.

Analyticals have but little time for small talk, and are impressed and convinced by thoroughness of approach. They feel reassured when all details are fully documented. Analyticals take time for particulars and will always seek to clarify specific points before moving on to the next issue.

The Expressive

Expressives need to be surrounded by people who are sharp and bright. They love ideas and creativity, but they can be slightly unstable, and even irresponsible in some instances. Expressive types like new approaches to solving their problems, and are attracted to breadth of thinking.

Expressives often have an artistic background and can be fairly unstructured in their own way of looking at things. They will fire questions in no particular order, and are not so interested in controlling a situation. In more rigid, inflexible organizations they may have difficulty in implementing their ideas.

The Amiable

The amiable type is a warm person who places a great deal of value on human relationships. Amiables will want to talk about family background, holidays, common relationships and other chatter before they are prepared to settle down to discussing business.

Amiables will put a great deal of emphasis on the quality of relationships, these being most important to them. They can easily get bored and do not like detail; they like the atmosphere to be light and amusing. Amiables will trust people readily until that trust is broken, when they can be quick to anger. They like to be invited to social functions, and they have a strong need to be liked.

Getting Along

There are important considerations to remember when working with people showing aspects of these four different styles. There are important do's and don'ts in adapting your own style to fit in with those around you; it is important to consider these when forming working relationships, whether you are in a superior, subordinate or equal position relative to your co-workers. To a certain extent most people adapt instinctively, but it can help to try and define who and what you are up against.

Dealing with the Driver

Drivers will have a high degree of ambition and will be very practical, moving into productive tasks rapidly. Loosely-structured organizations or ill-defined goals will cause them to be critical of their environment and to feel negative and bitter. Drivers will be independent in their work habits, and will want to achieve their objectives without delay. They may not easily conform to the rest of the organization, so it's important that their objectives match those of the company. Drivers can be difficult to supervise: desired results should be agreed in advance, and then the means to achieve them negotiated.

In relationships with others Drivers take charge even if it hurts someone else's feelings. They are often insensitive of the importance of understanding the attitudes and feelings of others. They must cultivate a willingness to be influenced by others and to listen, and should sometimes try to tone down their fierce independence. With respect to feedback and measurement of performance, Drivers should negotiate and use carefully-demarcated standards to measure their progress. Drivers need to be more humble, and must try harder to identify with the feelings of others.

When dealing with a Driver, you must be clear, specific and brief — and stick to business only. In making a proposal to a Driver, your package must be well-organized and presented efficiently, and you should provide alternatives and choices, with facts and figures about each option and all matters dealt with in a strictly impersonal way. If you disagree with a Driver take issue with the facts not with the person. By the same token should you agree with a Driver support the results achieved, not the person. Drivers need constant reference to objectives and outcomes. After discussing business with a Driver, leave the room quickly, otherwise you may be in danger of aggravating him or her and provoking his or impatience.

In a meeting with a Driver you must not ramble on or waste time; neither should you try to build a personal relationship. Do not be disorganized. You must not leave loopholes or vague issues or ask rhetorical or irrelevant questions. You should not approach a Driver with a ready-made decision, or speculate wildly and offer guarantees that may be uncertain. You should never try to convince a Driver by 'personal' means; neither should you direct or give a Driver an order.

Dealing with the Analytical

Analyticals will show great interest in structured activity. They like an orderly, systematic approach to life and they want to understand everything at issue. They will be responsive to a rational, well-organized environment. Analyticals may be highly academic in approach and critical of others whom they perceive to be less orderly. This tendency to be precise and to want clear logical answers all the time may annoy others, but Analyticals feel they must understand things in order to function correctly.

In their work habits Analyticals can overdo problem-solving to such an extent that they have difficulty making decisions and taking actions based on the available facts. They may be looking for more data when they should be making a decision, so they can tend to procrastinate; they must therefore be kept strictly to schedules. Analyticals may need to be encouraged to take more initiative and more risks in relationships with others, for they tend to be reluctant in these areas, fearing to impose their ideas on others.

Analyticals can be good listeners, but they tend not to take the initiative to build relationships. They would rather have people come to them than seek others out, and they like to use their problem-solving skills to help others arrive at decisions, rather than make these decisions themselves. Analyticals prefer the intellectual role of consultant rather than authoritarian positions. They need to learn how to reach conclusions and make judgments without delay, otherwise they will feel constantly under pressure. When the pressure gets too great Analyticals tend to slip into their back-up mode of procrastinating and avoiding action.

In dealing with Analyticals you should prepare carefully and approach them in a straightforward way. You should be supportive, using a thoughtful technique and gradually building up your credibility, listing the pro's and con's of each suggestion you make. You should appear to make an organized contribution to their efforts, taking your time and being persistent. With an Analytical, you should draw up a scheduled approach to implementing action, giving him or her time to verify the reliability of your action in each case. You should minimize the risk of their becoming dissatisfied with their performance by establishing a series of goals and rewards over a period of time.

With Analyticals you should not be disorganized, messy, casual, informal, nor loud; nor should you rush the decision-making process. You should not be vague about what is expected, and not leave things to chance. You should not threaten or cajole an Analytical, and you should not try to offer opinion as evidence. Analyticals do not like gimmicks or clever and quick manipulations. Analyticals should not be pushed too hard, or given unrealistic deadlines.

Dealing with Expressives

People with an expressive style will move into new situations readily, eager to please and willing to get involved even before they have a solid grasp of the situation. Expressives like exciting, fast-moving activities biased towards building relationships. They are not particularly concerned with details and do not always understand each step before moving on to the next. Expressives often try to say the right thing just to please others. Their work habits can be changeable, and they need an established track to follow.

Expressives are often not self-disciplined and have a tendency to generalize broadly, sometimes being imprecise in communicating facts. This can lead to misunderstanding in their dealings with others. Expressives should seek help in getting organized despite their in-built distaste for discipline. Relationships are very important to Expressives, and they frequently show concern about the feelings of others; they should however be careful not to lose their objectivity in their desire to forge relationships. They like status, prestige and social recognition, and they need constant inspiration and feedback. Expressives need to learn control and testing, verification and investigation procedures, as well as how to exercise self-discipline before taking action.

In talking with Expressives, you must support their dreams and intuitions, and not commit them to specific courses of action immediately. You should ask for their opinions about people and provide ideas to help them carry out decisions. You should leave time to socialize with Expressives, and try to be stimulating, fun-loving and fast-moving; being entertaining and in favour of quick action and risk-taking tends to appeal to them.

You should never lay down the law or suppress the opinions of Expressives. Don't be curt, cold, or tight-lipped. Don't concentrate on facts and figures or abstractions, nor go into too much detail. Neither should you, however, leave decisions up in the air. With Expressives, don't waste time trying to be impersonal, business-like and task-orientated, but don't go too far off-centre. Don't stick too rigidly to an agenda or be overly dogmatic, but don't talk down or patronize Expressives either.

Dealing with Amiables

Amiables are responsive to the leadership of others because they want to please the people they like. They can be co-operative but need direction to be effective. They work for attention, and conform to what is expected of them; they need structure and praise and want friendly, personal supervision. They can tend to defer the need to achieve objectives whilst establishing warm relationships. Amiables can thus seem lacking in initiative.

If you want them to establish a productive relationship with a specific task, they will need the support of others. Amiables can be persuasive and convincing, but they need details and specifics. Feedback is important, and Amiables need attention, but they also like to take risks. Take away the element of risk and you take away an Amiable's potential for growth, denying him or her the opportunity to experience the rewards of success and the exhilaration of achievement.

In dealing with Amiables you should break the ice with a personal comment, and don't fear showing a sincere interest in them as people. Look for areas of common involvement. You should be candid and open, patiently drawing out personal objectives and working together with the Amiable to achieve them. You should listen and be responsive, presenting your case non-threateningly. Asking 'how..?' questions will draw out their opinions — watch carefully for early signs of possible disagreement or dissatisfaction. If you disagree with an Amiable expect hurt feelings. You should behave casually and informally while still defining objectives clearly. Amiables need guarantees that their decisions will not increase risk, so you should give assurances and guarantees.

With Amiables you should never rush headlong into the agenda. Don't stick solely to business, nor should you lose sight of goals in your efforts to be personal. Don't force Amiables to respond quickly; don't be domineering or demanding; do not try to manipulate or bully them. Do not demean them by using subtlety, but don't be too abrupt. Don't be vague, nor offer too many options and probabilities. Don't keep deciding for them or they will lose their initiative. Do not leave them unsupported.

Putting It All Together

In your everyday dealings try to become more aware of the different types around you. See if you can categorize, even superficially, the types of people you deal with. For yourself, work on developing a variety of styles in order to accommodate as wide a range of people as possible. Adopt a chameleon approach. Decide which of the personalities you find it most hard to get on with, and make attempts to rectify this. In achieving your career turnaround you will inevitably have to get on with all types, and it helps to know how to prepare yourself.

It is now necessary to put this personal audit of yourself, together with the Mission Statement and Objectives you have developed thus far, into the broader context of the market in which you are operating.

SWOT Analysis: Market and Company Audits

Market Audit

A market audit when used to establish personal priorities and options takes the form of delineating what we can call push and pull factors. In order to be revealing these must be prefaced by a series of in-depth questions on the nature of your feelings about your current career and future prospects.

How did you come to enter your particular industry? Was it the result of accident or design, parental or peer pressure, or personal ambition? Is the business you are in now the one you would most want to be in if you could start again from scratch?

Think of yourself as married to your chosen line of work. If you suddenly discovered that the marriage wasn't legal, would you take steps to make it so or run while you had the chance?

Even if you were initially very enthusiastic about your field, are you still as excited by it? Does it still interest you as much as it did then?

When you are mixing socially, do other people envy your line of work or express their sympathies (or even criticism)? Are you proud of what you do or slightly embarrassed by it? How do your parents, your partner, your children or your oldest friends feel about it? Do they take the trouble to find out exactly what you do, or just assume it's fairly boring?

You may still be very committed to your selected area of work, but have become aware that it is in the doldrums, that it lacks the promise it may have had in the past, simply because of changing economics, or demographics, or whatever else it may be susceptible to.

Ask yourself the following questions: what it the current state of the industry I am in? Do I feel comfortable in this industry at this point in time? Do I think it is on the way up or on the way down? Is it keeping abreast with changes in related industries or is it falling behind? Is it only in a temporary, cyclical downturn, destined to rise again? Can I see on the horizon any great threats to the industry, such as legislative changes that might restrict my personal progress? How will I be affected by the increasing trend towards internationalization? How is the industry being changed by new developments in technology and communications?

Are there opportunities in your industry that you can capitalize upon, now and in the near future? How great is the competition? Will you still be able to make your mark, or will your contribution be inevitably lost among so many others? How can you position yourself to make the best of the possibilities on offer? Where do you fit in? Can you see any ways of making your role more visible and rewarding?

Can you apply all your best skills within this industry? You need to see yourself as a resource here, a benefit that can be applied in a variety of cases. Your skills and your individual approach are a unique combination of assets which should be used to garner the maximum possible return on your investment.

If your industry is changing, and you are feeling left behind, perhaps you need to enhance your assets more. Do you need to re-train or re-work your image to fit in better in your industry? Do you need to acquire new skills? How can you achieve this? Is there something you can do in your industry that you have never tried before, perhaps never even thought about?

It is not always necessary to leave your line of work entirely in order to achieve career turnaround. Most professions have a great variety of different areas, giving scope for various kinds of contributions.

How can you acquire skills that are in great demand? How can you divest yourself of skills that have become redundant? One way is to look around the confines of your industry, and take note of people you admire — what skills have they got? What work habits have they dropped? Try if you can to work more closely with these role models. Another way — and perhaps a more reliable one — is to take a course designed to help you gain proficiency in these new skills. Many companies are happy to support employees in this exercise; larger companies sometimes provide relevant courses in-house.

If you are not entirely happy in your industry, the solution may be to diversify your activities. You may have to retrench in one area and build-up in another. Alternatively you may have to leave your profession completely. The choice is yours, but you may want to take into account the following 'push factors':

- inability to make progress because of age
- job too dangerous
- limits to the contributions you can make
- no prospects for securing a top job in this field
- uncomfortable with the other people attracted to the business
- bored with being in the same field for so long
- dissatisfied with lack of variety
- industry no longer a young and exciting business
- inability to continue as the result of an accident
- lack of opportunities for advancement
- being made redundant
- reduced opportunities due to economic downturn

Various 'pull factors' can also exercise a powerful influence:

- prefer the independence of freelance lifestyle
- opportunity to make a mark by moving to new organization
- challenge of decision-making opportunities
- excitement of doing something completely different
- prefer shorter hours and more money
- chance to create a really worthwhile new business
- want a job involving travel, creativity, variety
- need scope for flexibility, variety, problem-solving, outside of a large corporate environment
- seek work that is more progressive and meaningful
- aim to be more entrepreneurial
- want to enter a new, exciting industry
- want to run a company, not just work for one

Which are more important to you, the push factors or pull factors?

Which are stronger? Which can you identify as being true of your own, present industry, or of the industry you might like to be in?

Company Audit

A market audit is an essential preliminary to a company audit; you may be in the right industry but in the wrong company. If you are in a large, stable, prestigious but rather unexciting company, perhaps you need to look for work in a smaller, more entrepreneurial one, or vice versa.

There are two aspects to your company audit: firstly, are you in the right company, and secondly, how well as you progressing in your company?

You must ask yourself if you are really at home in your company culture. The important point is that if you are operating in a company environment, you must have room within it to develop your career along the lines you want to. To some people this will mean going all the way to the top; for others, it will be a less responsible but perhaps more free and creative role.

What is your role in your company? Where are you now, and where do you want to be? Do you want to go all the way to the top, or will you be satisfied with a less lofty position? Do you think you have done quite well for your age, or are you being overtaken? Are there clear opportunities for promotion, or have you reached as far as you can go?

The Seven Roles of the Employee

Every organization includes seven types of employee, ranked according to their progress within that organization. A fundamental part of the career turnaround process is identifying your own point of progress and comparing it with others' both within your organization and outside it.

Similarly, when you enter a new area of business after implementing career turnaround, at what level are you coming in at? Is it markedly improved as compared to your previous level? At what level are your new associates working at? Do you have the potential to reach the highest level, or do you aspire to one that is not necessarily the highest but where you think you would be most happy?

Just as you need to understand and identify the four main personality types, you also need to understand and identify the seven main roles played by employees. Not everyone will assume each of the seven different roles during his or her working life, but will most likely experience at least two, one before and one after age 40. Taking up more than four roles is rare, as each role is linked to a certain personality type as well as to progress and motivation. Some will miss out the earlier stages, and others may miss those in the middle; inevitably, many will not make it to the top of the tree.

The seven different roles may be seen in terms of the roles played by movie actors. Salaries are of course relative, those given in the chart below will be earned in a sizable organization.

Under 40	**Over 40**
Young Hopeful	Character Part Player
Rising Star	Cameo Role Player
Matinee Idol	Guest Star

Mega Star

What are the attributes of those playing the different roles? What sort of positions do they hold? Of course, not all organizations will include these specific positions, but it should be possible to generalize to take account of a broad range of situations.

Young Hopeful

A typical Young Hopeful, aged 20-40, will be a young middle manager, salesman or assistant to a director, rising to the post of functional director, say in finance, sales, marketing or other line positions. He or she will clearly be doing very well, already on the high road. Young Hopefuls have leveraged their early training effectively, and have yet to experience any major failures, but maturity is still an issue. They will often be brash and perhaps rather one-dimensional in terms of their business experience. Frequently they have yet to realize their potential and be fully confident. Their attitude will be one of great optimism, not yet clouded by the perception of major obstacles in their climb to the top of the tree. They will be anxious to forge ahead, and may ride roughshod over slower people in their wake.

Rising Star

The 30- to 40-year-old Rising Star is commonly to be found in large middle management or functional director roles, leading up to Managing Director in a medium-sized business or Chief Executive in a smaller one. Rising Stars are clearly coming through very strongly indeed, having achieved more in business terms than they could have thought possible ten years ago. Rising Stars have also become politically dexterous within their organizations. They will probably be clocking up long hours at work, and not seeing much of their young families (if they've had time in the past to have them!). They are in danger of over-extending themselves, and must keep things in proportion. Rising Stars find it difficult to delegate, as their trust in others is still comparatively low. They have an excellent view of their market value, with a top-class business mind. They know how to put themselves in others' shoes, and how to work their way around an organization. Their concern at this stage is that they have enough qualifications and international experience to go all the way to the top. Many of the most effective and successful Chief Executives of Times 1000 and Fortune 500 companies will have been Rising Stars ten or twelve years before.

Matinee Idol

Having reached the position of functional director of a very large company, Managing Director of a medium-sized company or of a major division in a large company whilst still under 40, the Matinee Idol is the headhunter's dream. Earning a high salary at this comparatively young age, the Matinee Idol is probably poised on the brink of Mega Stardom and further success. Matinee Idols are truly ambitious, often to the point of ruthlessness. A sense of insecurity drives them to be still more and more successful. They are learning to develop the *gravitas* necessary to be a Mega Star, having overtaken early mentors. They are forging new values and top personal contacts, are clever at networking, and are clearly very high fliers indeed. Matinee Idols are classic high achievers, sometimes lacking a sense of humour, and are keen on cultivating their public image. They are often to be seen giving 'power lunches' and busily networking while still wanting to be liked and admired. They may be becoming even more concerned about their qualifications, their mastery of foreign languages, and their amount of international experience. Matinee Idols are good at team-building but increasingly intolerant of what they perceive to be failure around them. Fundamentally restless, Matinee Idols know they are smart and, having come so far, they definitely want to make it to the top.

Character Part Player

Character Part Players will be older than Young Hopefuls, approximately mid-40ish or even 50ish, but will have reached the same level in an organization and will occupy a similar position in the hierarchy. They may have peaked already, and may well be facing a mid-life re-evaluation which may or may not lead to career turnaround. They may have developed deeper non-work interests, seeing more of their families, and may be channelling their ambitions into their home and community lives. Character Part Players will be seen as a valued member of the team by their colleagues, but will feel that they would like greater recognition. They may feel they deserve this, but have not yet done a great deal to achieve this. They may feel boxed in, under-valued, and may decide that they cannot climb higher, choosing early retirement and a change in lifestyle. Character Part Players sometimes feel that they have lost control of their careers, and are becoming pessimistic and lacking in confidence.

Cameo Role Player

In their 40s and 50s, Cameo Role Players will have reached the same point as Rising Stars, but several years later. They will have achieved a great deal, and will probably make it to the upper reaches of the business community, but not necessarily all the way. Cameo Role Players know the headhunters well, have shown shrewd judgment of their own personal game plan and company politics, and are fairly pleased with what they have been able to achieve so far, although the next step is far from certain. Cameo Role Players are beginning to become concerned about younger people with equal or more ability coming through and overtaking them. In many cases they may feel that their rewards are not commensurate with their workload, and that they should be valued more. Cameo Role Players tend to concentrate on their strengths rather than their weaknesses, and would probably need considerable investment in training and management development to break out of this mould and progress to higher things.

Guest Star

Is the Guest Star, at the same senior level as the Matinee Idol but perhaps ten or more years older, going to make it to become a top Chief Executive, or has he or she peaked at this stage? Have Guest Stars suffered from a lack of opportunity, and if so, why? What is their real contribution to the performance of their businesses? Guest Stars have great strengths, but have not given enough thought to their weaknesses. They may be getting bored, not pushing themselves that extra metre, and may have tread the same ground over the last few years. They may be showing more concern for trade associations and non-executive directorships, which are diverting them away from the main task in hand. Guest Stars are often dreaming of a statesman role rather than aiming on improving and growing their businesses. They are frequently not entirely honest with themselves as to their true motivations and the effort and skill needed to achieve their goals. They realize that they may not have the energy for the top job, even if they were offered it. Their public image and identity can be diffuse and unclear.

Mega Star

There will be no doubt about a Mega Star, however. He or she will be independent in thought and action — a true leader, perhaps even a workaholic. All Mega Stars have robust personalities and considerable brainpower. They can often be idiosyncratic and egocentric, having worked very hard to achieve results. Mega Stars may appear mild on the outside, but on the inside they're like toughened steel. They are good team-builders, not extrovert in style, with a strong feel for success and how to achieve it. They show excellent judgment of a wide variety of people, and truly understand how to motivate people and put them in the right slot. Mega Stars know very well what they can and cannot tackle, and know themselves through and through. Mega Stars are often strong and very attractive personalities, with manifest weight and edge. They have achieved a strong public image and have no time for fiddle-faddle; for them, 'lunch is for wimps.'

Yet even Mega Stars can have nagging doubts, and no one is perfect. Can they repeat their early success? What is there now left to do? How can they remove some of the people around them whom they hired a few years ago and have now 'outgrown'?

Not everyone will want to be a Mega Star; nor does getting there mean you can stay there forever. Could you make it? Do you want to make it? For many, a career turnaround to become a Cameo Role Player or even a Character Part Player may be enough, and moving from Young Hopeful to Matinee Idol or even Rising Star may be as big a step as they want to make.

Your Company in its Market

Your personal progress within your company may be curtailed by the lack of progress your company is making in its market. If it is stagnant and conservative, your opportunities to rise into different roles will be severely limited. So, in analysing the role you have achieved in your company and how far you can go within it, you need to appraise the success of that company. If it's a winner then you will be. If it is falling behind in its market, then you may well find it impossible to realize your potential. You may well be in the right industry, but you may be in the wrong company, one that is not growing quickly enough. How does your company rank compared with its competitors? What do you think of it as a competitive force? This analysis should be taken into consideration when you are doing your market audit.

Next, you must endeavour to carry out some market research to ascertain how you can make the best of your assets.

Market Research

Phase One: Sought-after Qualities

Following your SWOT analysis, your market research should take two stages. Firstly you should find out which qualities are most sought-after in your chosen area of activity, and secondly you should consider your most influential role models — whom would you like to attract as mentors, and how can you go about approaching them?

Take a good look at your own and other industries. Where do your interests lie? Find out as much as you can about the field you'd like to move into: read trade magazines, go on courses, so that you can feel confident that you really know about what the market wants. Once you are aware of the qualities which are sought after by your chosen industry, you can develop your attributes to fit in with them. What are these qualities? Those described below have been shown by market research to be great assets for success in a variety of industries. Have you any of them in abundance? Developing them is an integral part of making sure that you are giving the market what the market wants.

Confidence

One of the most important features is confidence, a crucial element in career turnaround. Truly sought-after executives will always possess a special kind of confidence in their ability to overcome obstacles and succeed at anything they turn their hands to. They're

always going to come out on top in what they do; they are not troubled
with self-doubt. Obviously there is more than a touch of ego in their
make-up, but then one must try always to reinforce positive feeling
about one's talents and potential.

Clarity of Thought

Sought-after executives are blessed with a clarity of intellect and
presence of mind that allows them to see all the issues in an
uncomplicated, straightforward, clear and simple way. They do not
make simple issues complex. They synthesize complex issues into a
basic set of instructions so that other people understand — first time
— what there is to do, how to do it, and the goal to be achieved. They
define the world around them in a very concise way, and they are
masters of the art of the possible in seemingly impossible situations.
They turn first to their experience, clarity of thought and ability to
marshal facts and the issues; only after this do they ask questions.

Presentation

Another facet of these executives is how they look. Their self-image
comes across clearly. They are usually well-dressed. Often, but not
always, they are tall. They have great poise, and when you meet them
you feel immediately that you're in the presence of someone
meaningful, someone who is going to get things done. They have
charisma, often a touch of humour (but not overdone), and a no-
nonsense approach to things.

Knowledge, Experience and Opinions

Sought-after executives, when asked to discuss particular
opportunities and a particular company, will know about it already,
and they've typically got a view that can penetrate the central essence
of things quite quickly. For example, an outstanding personality in
the retail business was recently talking about another retailing firm.
He had formed the opinion that the firm wasn't going to last more
than six months: 'He's got to go, she's got to retire, the buffoon who's
the non-exec has got to disappear.' He had an extremely simple
diagnosis of what the issues were, and as things turned out he was
very nearly 100 per cent right.

Successful executives know they've only got a certain number of
changes they can make in their careers. They know the risks, they can

see the potential, but they balance the reward — the upside — with the risk, the downside. They've analysed themselves, so that they know precisely where their skills lie and where they're going to get into trouble, and what the balance of risk is.

They're sought-after because they impress. There are precious few people who have the experience, intelligence and strength that is theirs, and therefore they stand out, they are exceptional.

Potential

It can happen that certain young executives can be very sought-after despite their relative lack of experience. They will be appointed for their potential rather than their actual track record. Employers can be so impressed by these executives and their diagnosis of what needs to be done that they can 'fall in love' with them and hire them, therefore giving them a more influential job than they might otherwise have merited. These younger executives have to struggle to do the job, but they'll succeed because they are so talented and determined.

Such executives are very good at communicating, and have a distinct presence, sense of conviction, clarity and awareness of the issues as well as charm, sex-appeal, drive, and an innate sense of what to do. They are men or women of action — great to have around, and seen as stars of their company. All these characteristics come together in a cocktail that makes them really irresistible.

Drawing Power

Another aspect of those executives who are most sought-after is their power to attract other people of first-rate ability to work with them. They will not offer an easy ride, there may be a lot of difficulties as they go up and down the roller-coaster, but they're excellent mentors. They can bring in younger people very quickly indeed, inspiring tremendous loyalty, and they have the leadership skills that enable them to make an impact on other very good people. They're not often very good with second-rate people, however.

A very good executive will hire a team to support him- or herself, be its mentor, develop it, and introduce a number of excellent possible successors. An ideal situation is where you've got two or three successors, thereby leaving the executive board a real choice when the time comes for this sought-after executive to move on. The key result of the presence of a sought-after executive is that five years after he or she has left, the company is still thriving and growing, on course and going forward, because of the initial changes and success that he or she produced, and as a direct outcome of the legacy of continuity he or she has left behind. A gap will not have been left, because an able and competent successor will have been groomed to take over.

Diluting the Brand

Executives will no longer be sought-after if they have moved too often, because they will have diluted their expertise. The Grade-A executive will have an innate sense of when a move is right and when it's more prudent to stay. They don't job-hop. They're not so egocentric that they put themselves first — they won't leave until they've accomplished the goals they were hired to achieve.

Executive qualities emerge as a career develops. If an executive moves every two or three years, gaining no promotion with these changes in situation, then you can predict that his or her future will be the same, and that they don't really qualify as sought-after.

Today's Most Sought-After Attributes

The attributes that businesses are currently most looking for include top qualifications, international experience, and a facility for languages, all in a person of comparatively young age. Just as important as being formally qualified — a good first degree or MBA or post-graduate qualification — is solid experience gained at an early age with a good company. Sought-after executives have had the right sort of career development. Informed employers will know what this means: if he or she was with company x, he or she was mentored by y and moved on quickly by z.

If an executive has laid a good foundation for those early five or seven years, then he or she is prepared for career development into general management. Once the fundamental training has been acquired it is time to put the building blocks into place. Perhaps a person has spent time overseas, gaining a language or cultural skills. He or she may have worked in two or three different industries, spending time in a major consultancy, gradually broadening his or her experience and securing scope, breadth, imagination, knowledge, experience, and a rounded world view.

When such executives are confronted with a new and difficult situation, they will be able to solve many problems on their own initiative. It's usually a highly pressurized task to have to turn a business around or bring it forward, so they must be able to convince others that they have the inner confidence and emotional strength to make clear that the job, although huge, is still within their scope. Under pressure, these executives are not going to suddenly rush to the drinks cabinet or behave in ways they've never behaved before.

Other basic attributes of the sought-after executive include robustness and health, stability, the ability to minimize any tensions and to cope with a variety of pressures. This all comes out as a result of how one develops one's personality and the skills and experience one's gained en route.

Seeing the Big Picture

Most people react to a situation by looking for aspects with which they can identify personally, within their own experience; sought-after executives can put themselves into someone else's position. If they're so egocentric that they can only see themselves, they're not likely to be able to build a team or to understand the balance of loyalties. They've got to set the example — it's why they're sought out, because they've acquired maturity, wisdom, and a completeness of personality.

Many potential employers are looking for an executive whom they can contain within their own view of the situation, who will add vital input without taking over. The sought-after executive isn't just one type: they come in various forms. Some are in demand because of their clarity, their strategic brainpower, or their ability to be far-sighted. Sought-after executives know what they're good at, but more importantly know where they're weak, and know how to firm up those weaknesses.

Executives who are really good at operating within a structured company strategy can also be extremely sought-after because they know exactly what they're going to do, what they're good at, and where the balances are, and they don't look to less possible horizons. There's no point in putting a marketing strategist into a job where the object is to control and cut costs, to make do with what's there. Successful money management requires completely different skills.

A pre-requisite of the sought-after executive is to be politically sensitive. Anybody in an organization of any size must know when to back off and when to come forward, when to go after something aggressively and when to placate. Those devoid of these skills would never have come so far in the first place.

Talent doesn't come in just one size or form; it's multi-dimensional. But being sought-after means that you do not allow yourself to be sought-after by everyone, you must maintain an aura of exclusivity.

Which of your qualities will be most sought-after in your preferred company and/or industry? Which could be most valuable to you? Which should you beef up or tone down?

- self-assurance
- slight egotism
- clarity of intellect
- presence of mind
- ability to synthesize complex issues
- good dress sense
- charisma
- no-nonsense approach
- up-to-date market knowledge
- confidence
- impressive demeanour
- knack for attracting others to work with you
- distinctive style
- adaptability, especially to different cultures
- awareness of not diluting the brand
- a well-structured career
- top-quality qualifications
- top-quality experience
- top-quality mentors
- team-building abilities
- capacity to see the whole picture
- understanding of the balance of loyalties
- maturity
- consolidated wisdom
- completeness of personality
- emotional stability

- ability to play a support role
- self-knowledge
- talent for thinking creatively and strategically
- ability to work to a prescribed strategy
- political sensitivity
- exclusivity

A shorter version of this article, by John Viney, was published in *First* magazine, vol. 4, no. 4, 1990.

Phase Two: Cultivating Mentors

Following on from your market research into the most sought-after qualities, the next step is to put your plans and ambitions into action. Cultivating mentors is an important way of using your market research to aid your personal advancement. In order to progress in a company or industry, you have to network with the right people. A vital part of your market research strategy will be finding out who these people are, and how to use this information to your best advantage.

A mentor is probably a great prize, and not everyone is lucky enough to have one. If you haven't had one in the past or haven't got one now, you've got to cultivate one. Most people, when they think of mentors will remember influential role models from school, college or university, or from their first job. You now have to find someone like this, someone who can help you achieve your career turnaround.

Early and Mid-Career Mentors

Some early mentors can be held in high esteem for most of your life. You can probably still relate to them; you might look back on a mentor, now quite old, about whom you can still say 'He started me on the road, he's extremely good and I learned a lot from him.' But the mentor who helps in a mid-career turnaround is not necessarily the same sort of mentor at all.

Say you're in a mid-career situation and there's someone you really admire in your company. You want to make strides forward and you think he or she can help you, but you don't know the person very

well. How can you win his or her confidence and get him or her to
help you? It's often a different thing entirely from the sort of mentor
who influenced you at college. In a corporation difficulties arise as a
result of perceived obstacles between you and the mentor him- or
herself. Others in the company might think you're 'sucking up to the
boss.' This is one of the dangers, but it's not an insuperable one.

Attracting a Mentor

One of the ways of attracting a mentor is to find out what this prize
creature does for recreation. Is he a golfer? If so, join the same club.
Try to see him away from the office. Does his wife work with yours?
Do your kids go to the same school as his? Try to explore as many
avenues of contact as you can.

A best-selling American guide to being headhunted, *The Career
Makers* — gives classified information on the out-of-office activities
of all the top headhunters, such as their sports, hobbies, clubs and
recreational endeavours. Unfortunately for UK or European readers
there is no equivalent. You'll have to do your own homework. It need
not be difficult. The important thing is to try to get to know your
potential mentors on a personal level, in an easier, more relaxed
environment than within the corporation.

First Contact

Another approach is to go up to this influential person and just say
something straightforward, but in a casual way, such as 'I don't want
you to think I'm sucking up to you, but I would really like to take you
out to lunch, away from here — not in the staff canteen — because
I'd like to understand a few things about where I am and where I'm
going to, and you seem to me to be someone who has a very
successful career. You do many of the things I would like to do, and
I would love it if you could find the time for me to nicely pick your
brains.'

You buy her lunch, you've got her there — but plan it very carefully.
Plan what you are going to talk about, what you want to know. Ask
yourself, 'How must I seem to this person?' This is a very important
opportunity on the road to career turnaround. You don't want your
would-be mentor to perceive you as a pathetic and useless character;
you want to be recognized as someone who's genuinely trying to
develop skills and make progress in a carefully-planned and
thoughtful way.

Most people would be surprised at how willing very senior, accomplished and influential executives are to be mentors. They may have chosen the same route themselves, and feel quite obliged to their mentors, and see one way of returning the favour as being a mentor to someone else. Even a chief executive who's obviously much admired by many people, the sort of character who receives a lot of publicity, may well be prepared to guide a young or mid-career executive who seriously wants his or her career to take off at greater speed. Such an executive would probably be quite impressed that someone actually had the temerity to approach him or her for help.

Very good people often give up time to people on the way up; they're conscious that they were once on the way up themselves. And there's always the flattery aspect, remember; because a lot of these people in top positions are not without ego — they're vulnerable to a little flattery. Even between two men or two women flattery is a useful and effective tool. Also, they are more than likely astute enough to know that they'll learn from you nearly as much as you'll learn from them.

Taking people who are apparently more successful out to lunch and showing an ability to be able to get close to them is a skill that can be learned. It requires practice and careful preparation. You must seek focused, specific advice on what you want to achieve, constantly referring this back to what the prospective mentor has achieved, showing that you have followed their career closely. How you handle this meeting is one of the crucial steps on the way to achieving career turnaround.

Dos and Don'ts

Do talk about yourself and what you have achieved so far — not too modestly nor flippantly, but to indicate that you've been trying to go forward and are conscious of the fact that you've missed something somewhere, that you need help to maximize your potential. You have to demonstrate that you are capable of helping yourself, that all you need is someone to point you in the right direction. This doesn't just mean acquiring more contacts, it means increasing your level of awareness of what you can do and what it takes to do it.

And also it would be a good tack just to ask a simple question, such as 'Perhaps you could tell me how you got to where you are now?' This is not only ego-boosting for the would-be mentor, but of practical help and interest.

A person who is determined to achieve career turnaround will take an interest in how other people have accomplished it, and will remember the stories of the way in which successful people got to where they are now. It's usually highly relevant, but is mostly ignored. It's important to be able to spot patterns in what other people have done and how they were motivated, in order to work out how you can achieve the same kind of satisfaction and success. The case studies that make up the last chapters of this book are offered as examples of successful paths to career turnaround.

Presentation

In approaching your prospective mentor you may find you need to put yourself across more effectively. The decision to try a career turnaround is of itself an admission that you need to develop new skills: communication is the first talent you'll want to refine. Your mentor is one of the first people you have to convince of your seriousness in desiring a career turnaround, and if you can't put yourself across to him or her, you have little chance of facing the rest of the world in a new role.

One aspect of presenting yourself is assertion. Being assertive is a skill which can be gained through training. It doesn't mean being pushy, or shouldn't do: it means showing the world that you know what you want, and that you have some confidence in how you're going to get it. Many people find that they can become more assertive as they grow in confidence, as the process of their career turnaround unfolds.

One very important part of putting yourself across is how you sound. Do you sound hesitant and unconvincing, not because of the content of what you're saying, but because of your style of delivery? Listen to the professionals on radio or television. To have more impact, they have learned how to modulate their voices, so that they don't sound jerky or discordant, neither do they sound monotonous. Also, remember to speak in shorter sentences; one idea per sentence. Make sure you have finished each point before you start another. Speak in a direct, simple and sincere way, brief but not clipped. Sound purposeful, with the conviction that you have a mission; don't forget grace or humour.

Humour should not be overdone, however, and should be tailored to one's audience. Some people are quite offended by crude humour, and you don't want to be remembered just as someone who tells good jokes. Let your sense of humour add to your attractiveness, not detract from it.

It is important to put over to your mentor a slight feeling that you're going to do more in the future than you've done today, to give a hint of your potential. All these things together — enthusiasm, assertiveness, determination, being articulate with a sense of fun — may sound a heady mix. But you can do it, you have within you all these things, and to convince your mentor to take you under his or her wing you must demonstrate them all.

Imagine that your first meeting with your would-be mentor is like going on a blind date. You're rather nervous, of course. Your first reaction might be to come out in a sweat at the thought of actually having to go out on this blind date. You may think you'd want to drink yourself under the table to be able to cope with it. In the same way as in a blind date, you'll have to establish if there's any attraction — not necessarily in a physical sense — whether there's any chemistry there. You've got to make your mentor want to establish a fairly close relationship with you as someone who's interesting, going places, and having something to offer.

You've got to appear conscious that every day is different and that you appreciate and make the most of opportunities. Although you must appear assertive, it ought to be re-emphasized that you mustn't appear too pushy, you should seem to be relaxed. Otherwise, the would-be mentor will feel on edge. You haven't got to appear under pressure. You can be quite purposeful without appearing desperate.

Maintaining Contact

You've got to decide whether or not you want to pursue this person as your mentor. Is he or she right for you? Do you like him? Is there any rapport there? Will she inspire you to achieve your goal? Will he be able to spare the time to help you? You must be sure at this point, because disillusionment later could be very damaging.

On the other hand, if your prospective mentor has decided that for some reason he or she's not particularly struck with you, you've got to be able to read the signs and take the hint. For example, imagine the advertising executive trying to get you to use his advertising company. He prepares some sample work, sends all the brochures, and comes and docs a presentation. But then you decide that maybe you don't really like him that much after all, you don't think the people you're working with will like him, you know he's done all this stuff but you don't really like it, it's all a bit too much. So you say something like 'I think we want to change the spec, and we want something much more simple and basic and just informative.' But instead of saying 'OK, I understand, perhaps another time,' he says 'Oh I'll do that just as easily, whatever you want.' So you say, trying to remain tactful, 'But we don't need anything so creative, it's all meant to be a bit low-key, and doesn't really need your talents.' But he persists, saying, 'Oh, that's all right, I'll do it.' At this point you will be asking yourself why he is so desperate. You try one last tack: 'You don't want to work for us really, we change our minds all the time and don't pay the bill at the end.' If he says 'Oh, I'm sure you're all right really' to this, you know you shouldn't have anything more to do with him.

If however your would-be mentor doesn't try to turn you off, and clearly likes you, you must keep in touch. Follow that lunch up with other meetings, both formal and informal. You must convince him or her that you're around to help if ever he or she needs you, and keep him or her well-supplied with interesting and useful information. You must bear in mind the *quid pro quo* aspect of having a mentor.

Checklist:

- Attract a mentor
- Make first contact, if possible *outside* the office
- Don't be afraid to use flattery
- Present yourself successfully
- Sound purposeful
- Have a sense of humour
- Be aware of any opportunity
- Don't be too desperate
- Keep in touch
- Be prepared to help your mentor

Product Development: Creating Your Own Brand

By now you will have completed your SWOT self-analysis, carried out the necessary market research on the qualities most in demand in your chosen field, and gained the help and support of a mentor and peers. Next you need to approach the problem of marketing yourself.

In successfully carving out a new career for yourself, you've got to project an image that is different from anyone else's. It's a hard thing to do, but you've got to make what you're selling unique: quite simply, you've got to create a brand name and reputation. First you've got to have a commodity, then you've got to make it distinctive.

Examples of Commodities Turned into Brands

To take an example: oil, used to lubricate car engines. You may say oil is oil is oil: it comes out of the ground and is put to all different kinds of uses in industrialized countries throughout the world. And yet in the UK two companies have branded oil: one is Castrol and the other is Shell. In the USA, you will see Mobil and STP brands as well. One company will try to convince you their oil has got special benefits to your car over and above all other oils. It is attempting to make a brand out of a commodity.

The company have not necessarily altered the commodity drastically, and hopefully it's as good as any of the others. They say 'We've put a little bit of this in, and we've done this, and we package it like this, and promote it like this, so this is a *brand*.' A brand usually has a bigger price tag, and if you've been convinced that it's better than its competitors, the company will have succeeded in adding value to the brand.

Differences between brands can be very subtle indeed. Take another example: bottled mineral water. If you were to blindfold people and ask them to taste ten different mineral waters most people wouldn't be able to tell one from the others. And yet given the right packaging — a pleasantly-shaped bottle, for example — people will swear that one brand is superior to the others.

People as Brands

What people contemplating career turnaround have got to do is to understand that their skills are a commodity and that they've got make themselves more special. They have got to make themselves into a brand.

This is what good salespeople do. If you're in a creative business, you have to make your work and your contribution so unique that it is instantly recognizable as yours, even without your name on it. If it's written work, for example, people should be able to read it and realize who wrote it, not only because of its content, but because of its style. It should have a value because of the person who wrote it, reflecting that person's authority and knowledge. This will increase its credibility.

The Benefits of Branding

Branding accomplishes more than just lending credibility to a product: it gives confidence to both the buyer and the seller. As confidence in a product increases so too can its cost. Some people pretend to be totally impervious to brands yet still make a point of ignoring them. Brands are becoming an increasingly important feature of everyday life, and are used as a very effective way of achieving competitive leverage. In the same way that certain items on the supermarket shelves are more successful and more profitable than others, people can use the idea of promoting themselves as a brand in their own careers to carve a niche for themselves.

Another illustration of the confidence that successful branding can engender is in the cat food market. The makers of cat foods realized early on that pet owners do not want to give their cat something that's not of the highest quality. One company in particular have pushed home this notion of not settling for 'second best', and it is this company which leads the market. There are many more examples of a brand making a tremendous difference to profit margins and helping to exclude the competition. In terms of the pet food market, once a brand has caught the buying public's imagination these buyers tend not to shop around, they buy the same kind every time. Catering for cats, who are promoted as being more 'fussy', has been taken into account as well — the leading pet food company offers a range of products for cats, offering different menus and thereby keeping hold of those punters. A good brand will develop and adapt according to people's wants and desires. And of course different brands appeal to different markets — there's a world of difference between the tactics used by tabloid and quality newspapers: they understand their respective markets and advertise accordingly. You must make yourself a student of brands and the markets they're aimed at.

Stretching the Brand

One way of adapting is to try to widen a brand's appeal. For example, confectionery companies have recently begun selling ice-cream variations of their already well-known and well-established chocolate bars. What they have done is to try and broaden their sales base. It's called stretching the brand. If your brand seems not so successful, what is needed might not be a total revamping of what you have to offer but merely this kind of expansion. You must ask yourself some questions: How far can a particular brand be stretched? Can a service brand be expanded to include other services? Brands do not cover everything. Just because you trust a certain brand for its washing powder does not mean you will trust them if they branch out into toothpaste.

The most important thing to establish is a sense of quality: once your brand has a reputation for this you may be able to expand its resources indefinitely. This is another aspect of having successfully established a brand: you have a base of loyal customers, a captive market if you wish for future products, eliminating a great deal of the risk involved in trying to branch out into new areas.

Improving the Brand

Even with the most successful brands, they often stay basically the same. It is important to instil in your buyers/clients the idea that your product is being continuously improved. Perhaps evolving is a better word.

Some companies will change a brand's logo to keep up with the times. They evolve subtly, adding slight changes over time. When brands are developed and enhanced in this and other ways they have a clear value almost independent of the company that produces them.

Revitalizing and Restoring a Brand

Brands can be negative as well as positive, and can be damaged. But you can revitalize brands, and there have been many examples of new life being breathed into a brand that has been on the rocks. One example is Thomas Cook, one of the oldest-established travel agencies in the world. It was very successful as an independent company, then it was taken over by British Rail. They tried to subsume the brand into their own marketing, but you can't keep a good brand down. Now it has been made part of the British Midland Bank Group, and the brand has been revived.

Even if there has never been any goodwill associated with a brand in the past there is still scope for its revival, especially if it can be marketed as capturing the ethos of a bygone age. Often just by being around a long time a brand can seem established and reputable.

Brands that are not known for very good quality, however, will never inspire any confidence in the consumer. If a product is no good, you'll never be able to market it as a brand. This goes for your personal brand as well. Good marketing and promotion are important, but the product has to be high-quality.

Recruiting Help for Restoring a Damaged Brand

It's comparatively easy to attract good people to a well-known, blue-chip company with a good track record of performance and growth. By contrast, it is a great challenge to attract good people to rescue a company that has shown a downturn in performance and has gained a poor image among executives in the marketplace. The very last solution which a company in a bad patch needs is mediocre people, but often these are all they can attract.

There are five strategies or options for attracting good people to a less than successful company, people who can help restore that company's fortunes. The first three of these strategies capitalize on the fact that there are under-utilized elements of the workforce who are capable of rising to a challenge.

1.   Target younger executives. Offer them a job that is two sizes too

big for them, and hope that they will grow into it, given encouragement and support from a highly-motivated chief executive and from supportive team mates.

2. Approach older executives, who may be of the opinion that having established themselves they have little to lose from an association with a company whose reputation is a bit damaged. They may have become bored with the routine of their lives, and may be attracted to the challenge of a new opportunity.

3. Look at minorities, including women, who are rarely offered opportunities and who may respond to the challenge because they appreciate the opportunity more than those who are frequently approached, and who will try especially hard to make it into a success.

4. Get in touch personally with foreign candidates who might be interested in working in the UK.

5. Offer good money. There are many people who will take the risk of an attempted turnaround if the financial rewards are attractive enough.

Through the attraction of quality executives (younger or older than the norm, from minority groups, from overseas, or — comparatively rarely — through paying a premium), many brands can be restored, and can go on to attract more and more of the best people.

If a brand is in trouble there can be great sums involved in effecting its recovery. It is most important that second-rate candidates be avoided. These people could be supported and encouraged by a strong brand, but they will inevitably make a weak brand weaker still, so that it may never recover. A company with a damaged public image, suffering poor performance, needs a strong and able executive with the courage to examine the company's internal structure, its pay policies, products and service. Such an executive must achieve change and improvement without harming any positive elements with which the company is graced.

Branding and Individual Career Turnaround

For people looking to establish a successful reputation in a new business there are many lessons to be learned from the marketplace. People can be brands, putting their brand trademark on all they do.

Brands are enhanced by reputation, knowledge and experience, but what a lot of people don't understand is that a brand can also be diluted. You must beware of becoming too complacent or smug about your brand, or of spreading yourself too thin. Stick to emphasizing your most positive traits and talents.

In corporate turnarounds, enhancing and capitalizing on brands is very important indeed, and just as companies seeking turnaround pay more attention to sales and marketing, persistently polishing and improving their brands, so should you. Try always to cultivate and develop your strengths, continually adapting to changing market forces and consumer demand.

A good brand can improve the people working for it. If you associate yourself with a good brand, it may well have the effect of lifting the quality of your work. The customers will have a preconceived notion of quality, and this in itself can improve your approach. Conversely, it is much harder to work for a company with a poor, weak or tarnished brand, and these companies require more able people to be successful. In terms of your own personal brand, it must be one you can live with comfortably, one which is right for you. If you're just a bit old fashioned by nature, than your brand can be an old-fashioned one, as long as it stresses the positive aspects of being classic, enduring, established and based on a tradition of quality, rather than being fuddy-duddy, behind the times, outmoded and inefficient.

A brand that is a pretence cannot be sustained, as in the case of the Gilbert & Sullivan character who admits he's an aesthetic sham, trying to appear pure and deep but secretly feeling bored and restricted by the whole performance. You've got to be who you are, but this does not mean you cannot adapt. You can make apparently unattractive features more attractive, as in the case of someone who's seen as being a bit uncouth — this feature expressed differently will be seen as directness and honesty. The important thing is to decide what you want your brand to be like, and then work hard to achieve it. Remember: you are unique — just make sure people know you are!

Once you have established what you see as a unique brand for yourself, then you have the problem of how you go about selling it to people. At this point, you should realize the vital difference between marketing and selling. Selling is getting someone to buy what you have, and marketing is creating in response to consumer demand. You will be selling your brand, but you will be marketing it as well. You can sell what you've already got, but you must also try to make yourself into someone people want.

Matching the Benefits

Now what you have to find out about — and this is your sales role — are those things that address your customers' needs. So, as in the case of consumer product selling, you have to address your market with questions about their needs, and then try to equate these needs with the features that are part of your brand. This is called matching the benefits.

To take the mineral water analogy again, you may point out to your potential customer that he or she might be very interested in your brand of mineral water because it fits in his or her fridge easily, or looks very nice on the dining room table, or actually has the right chemicals and minerals for enhancing his or her health.

Before you know which feature of your brand is going to be most important, you've got to find out more about your potential customers. So you'll be interested in finding out things about their particular lifestyle. Is healthy eating important to them? Knowing that your customer is very keen on health, you might say 'this is a great product to have in the fridge when you get home after a three-mile run, because it not only quenches your thirst — big plus I would think after you've run so far — but also has the mixture of minerals there to replace what you've lost.'

Different features will appeal to different people, and your job as a salesperson is to find out which features appeal to which people, and target them accordingly. This has got nothing to do with price, it's to do with need. If I can make the case that I can fulfil a very strong need for you, then you'll buy it, almost regardless of the price. That's what a salesperson tries to do, and the parallel here is that when you are trying to sell yourself in a new role, as part of your career turnaround strategy, you've got a number of features which you can highlight. You're in possession of many attributes that you can list — strong, attractive features, not just that you're 6'1" or an attractive 5'5", but skills, experience, knowledge, abilities, and qualifications. If you make a list of your features you can then understand which aspects you can emphasize. The trick is to pluck those features which are most attractive — the thing you want to become — and sell them as benefits to your potential customers.

You've got to know your benefits and be able to identify which ones to accentuate to the person you've targeted. That's what the good salespeople do.

Singling Out Your Unique Feature

You should emphasize your unique qualities, thereby distinguishing yourself from other, competing brands. This is the key element of advertising. People, the consumers, will be the recipients of any benefits you have to offer, and as such should be the focus of all your market research.

The advantage your particular traits offer won't necessarily be unique for very long. Others may try to copy your success. You should therefore always keep a careful eye on the competition, comparing your features to those of others. You must ask yourself what makes you different. What have you got that allows you to charge more or expect more people to come to you to answer their particular needs?

You should always be looking out for those things that make your product unique. Then take those things that make your product unique and try and find people who will benefit from them. Similarly, in a personal way, you've got to say 'Well, what have I got that others haven't? What am I good at that other people are not? Why should someone choose me to do this?'

You don't necessarily need dozens of features to make you stand out from the crowd. You only need *one feature* to distinguish yourself or your product. The trouble with some people is that they think the hard sell will work: they shove every feature in sight and every benefit they can think of at their customers, taking no notice of each person's individual needs. In reality it takes only one difference to separate yourself from your competitors. But you need to be able to recognize that one difference and be able to present it successfully to your market.

Gathering Market Intelligence

It is also valuable to be able to see what the competition is doing and to understand what you're doing in this context. You must know at any given time what your competitors are doing, what they are charging, whom they're working for.

Surprisingly, most people are uninterested in what the competition is doing. They're either rather smug, feeling that they don't have to worry about what anyone else is doing, or they imagine they are too busy getting on with their work to notice or care what anyone else is up to.

If you manage to collect market intelligence, then you are in a very strong position to manoeuvre your brand into better positions, into new areas that no one else has thought of. You will be ahead of the game. It also gives you the confidence to get in there and compete. You know the competition's strengths and weaknesses, and you know your own: using this knowledge is the way you win the business.

Creating a Need for Your Brand

So you're in a new career and are perhaps lacking a bit in confidence at the beginning because you are not yet completely comfortable with your new endeavour. You've got to prove yourself, but at first you don't know the competition. You've got to know what you're up against. Before you can establish a brand you have to learn as much as you can about the business you've entered, understanding it as a commodity. You have to work out what is important for you to know, but you also have to be able to offer something special that no one else has, something that has come out of your own unique experiences, background and intelligence.

You know that what you have is the same information, the same basic raw material that everyone else has, but you must also realize that you have the ability to take this basic material and make it extra special, because you can interpret the need for it in the market in a distinctive and unique way.

You then refine and develop those personal features that you have and the competition lacks. Before you decide on the main strengths of your brand, analyse what you have that is really unique, and centre your brand around this. Stage two is finding punters to whom your added features will appeal, i.e., matching the benefits. Features only become benefits when they meet a need in the market. If there is no need for it — if no one is thirsty they won't want any mineral water, no matter how great it is — no one will want to bother, they won't even look at you.

Needs come out of people's individual psychology — that's why we buy different things. Mineral water was hardly heard of ten or fifteen years ago. How was this need created? The emphasis on designer goods, as well as a genuine interest in offsetting the effects of pollution, have created a niche in the marketplace for the successful sale of mineral water.

Reviving an Interest in Your Brand

Many companies undergoing corporate turnaround have had to recreate a need for their brand. Take British Airways, for example. There is clearly a need for a national airline, but if there is a choice of others and they're better, people will go to them. So British Airways had to create a new 'need', based on a new brand.

The revival of a brand means the recreation of a brand. It's all a matter of being able to follow and to some extent anticipate changing tastes and styles. As always market research is very important. In the case of British Airways, a huge amount of research was carried out, and to this day they routinely enact research, for example on what annoys people about waiting for tickets or any other features of their service.

Using In-depth Market Research

What can make all the difference, and the element that can make your brand more successful than anyone else's, is the depth of your understanding of your market. The Japanese are excellent at plumbing the depths of market research, exploring areas which no one else has ever thought of. For example, one of the Japanese car manufacturers undertook research that almost amounts to a form of industrial espionage.

They hired a Japanese student and sent him to the USA for a year, with the instructions that he was to live with an American family (while studying at an American university). They would pay all his bills, all he had to do in return was watch the family and try to get involved in every aspect of their lives. He was to ascertain their need for a car, studying exactly how they used it, where they took it, their storage needs, etc. This student did as instructed, reporting back to the company and enabling them to design a superbly practical family car.

Above all, you've really got to understand the needs of your customers in the broadest possible sense before you can hope to gain acceptance of the new you and of any innovations that you're trying to achieve.

The matter of networking has been raised before, but its link to the concept of branding needs to be examined in more detail. Getting to know what your customers' needs are is one form of networking, but actually attracting new customers and building up your established brand is another, more refined aspect, and one that is just as important.

One part of this networking is finding people who need you or your product and the skills that you have developed. You've got to network until you find the people who can most appreciate and use your unique features.

Building on Established Networks

One of the important things that can help you stand out is your past experience. Your skills, potential and image, and the way they are associated with your previous or early career, can all go towards lending you distinction. Getting people to want to work with you is one of the requirements for establishing credibility in your new career. Of course you can't expect to succeed in every case, and you won't appeal to everybody, but you must build on your past experience to network with those who can help you. Use your old brand to help build a new one.

You're in a new position and you want to prove yourself and gain recognition. You will be aware of the definitions of quality work and success in your previous role, the top brands associated with this, and how people within these certain brands were outstanding. You will need to find the arbiter of quality in your new business. Is it formal or informal? Which are seen as the leading brand names? How do people network? All professions and occupations are subject to ratings and a pecking order; all have brands that are stronger than others. Recognizing this was one of the ways in which you built up credibility in your previous role. Now you must start again from scratch, learning to recognize it in your new career.

Networking Through Brand Association

Networking is made much easier if you are already associated with good brands. A good brand is not only a good company you may have worked for; it can also be a good college or university. If you look carefully over your personal history there are sure to be many points of contact with quality organizations or individuals.

Don't expect to be able to build on the same brand forever, though. You've got to do other things and make new associations rather than forever harking back to college days or resting on laurels now withered with age. A person may benefit initially from the brand recognition of a college or university but if they fail to make progress they will impress no one. You must enhance your own value over and above your antecedents.

Trading Down on the First Brand

It's not enough to think you can just network all your life on the basis of the first brand with which you were associated. You mustn't give the impression that this is as far as you can get, for after a while people will no longer take an interest in you. It's no good to show early promise and then let it die. There are those who try to live off trading on the first brand they were associated with, without developing ties with further brands or adding to this initial asset in any way.

There is a corporate analogy here: it's like a failure to invest and further expand the potential of an acquisition. An important aspect about marketing is that you must keep investing in the brand. You must find new ways of adding value and sustaining its ability to attract people: new variants, better advertising, more attractive packaging. If you don't continue to add value to the brand, failing to invest any more time or money into it, then the brand becomes tarnished, and the asset a positive liability.

Trading Up on the First Brand

People who do not know how to enhance their own value lose the brand and any benefits of their association with it. Potential customers are quick to smell defeat and will abandon anyone who has failed to capitalize effectively on the brand.

It has to be a continuous process. It's as if a company with a strong brand, with all the benefits of being first in its field, suddenly relinquishes this status. If we look at what happened to Rank Xerox, who lost market share heavily after being market leaders for so long, and who are now trying to reclaim their place, they've realized that they can never relax again. They enjoyed an amazing position — they had a monopoly on reprographics, and the patent. When the patent expired they lost their monopoly position. It was no longer the case that they would be market leader irrespective of their product or performance. While they had the monopoly they used it to advantage; when they lost it they didn't know what to do.

Building on the First Network

A good brand will give you an instant network, which can be very supportive and comparatively unquestioning. You can milk a brand for a certain amount of time, but not forever. You have to give something back, to add to your brand. There are very few people with a truly unique product; many other people will have the same basic one. Adding to the brand in your own individual way is what makes it unique. Once a brand is known among a particular network you can work to increase its value. Your first network will provide you with a ready-made group of clients or customers who will be predisposed to accept any new brands you create. It's akin to using a brand as an 'old-boy network': it has its uses, but they are limited. By all means use it, but add to it, develop it, extend it, and think beyond it.

Now that you have thought through the processes of mission statement, forming objectives, SWOT analysis, market research, finding a mentor and developing your personal product into a brand, you are ready to implement all your plans and hopes, devising a strategic plan that will put your original objectives into action.

Reviewing Objectives

Reviewing your objectives is an important stage in the marketing plan. Inevitably your objectives may have to be re-thought out or adjusted after examining the market and carrying out your personal audit.

Look back at your original objectives. Do they seem too ambitious, or not ambitious enough? Of your seven goals relating to your working and personal life, which do you now feel it is most appropriate for you to concentrate on? Do you now feel in a better position to prioritize them in a different order?

After your personal audit, do you feel more encouraged by your newly-discovered abilities and qualities, or less so? It may be necessary to adjust your objectives accordingly. After your market audit, do you feel that you should perhaps stay in your current industry, or are you more determined than ever to break away? After your company audit, does your firm appear better and more attractive than you thought, or even worse?

This and your market research will help you to further refine your objectives and prepare them for implementation.

Implementing Career Turnaround

You should now have all the information you need to build up a clear strategic plan, and a shrewd idea of how to put it into action. At this point you need to develop a personal campaign, with reference to your earlier objectives. You know where you want to go, whether this means

- defining a new job specification,
- changing your role,
- joining a new company, or
- becoming part of a different industry.

Implementing your career turnaround will require:

- Networking and cold-calling
- Making initial contact
- Being a good listener
- Building confidence
- Getting headhunted:
  why the headhunters can help you
  being interviewed by a headhunter
  how not to impress a headhunter
  how to attract a headhunter

Networking and Cold-calling

Effective networking is critical to a successful career turnaround. You've got to go and seek the advice of those who are doing what you want to do or have done what you want to do, and you have to use the subtle approach. You can't go in saying 'Look, can you help me or not?' You'll get a lot further if you say 'Look, I need your advice, and I'd like to know what you think has made you successful, how you've got where you are today.'

Britons have a great fear — unheard of in their American counterparts — of just picking up the telephone and ringing someone up 'cold'. Practically no one — say 99 out of 100 people — would be willing to make cold calls. Yet good, able, successful people tend to have good egos, and egos can be massaged. They would probably be most flattered if you were to ring and ask to speak with them for a few moments, gleaning any information you could about their experience.

Cold-calling may seem a terrifying idea, but effective career turnaround means having to accept that you're going to have to do it. Accepting it is one thing — actually doing it is another. The good news is that a lot of people are more accessible than you might have thought. After all, how do they stay on top unless they are out there willing to listen to new ideas? The person you contact will also benefit: it's all part of networking, and a very important part at that. A successful cold call will result in a new ally, mentor or even friend, and perhaps a referral onto someone or something else. One call often leads to another, and so on.

If you can't quite see yourself being able to do any cold-calling, then the next best thing is to write a letter ahead of time, stating in it that you will be following the letter up with a phone call within a few days time — be as specific as you can, it will show the person that you are organized and serious about your intent to speak to them. In some instances cold letter-writing is more acceptable and more likely to produce results.

Planning Your Approach

Obviously you can't always go straight to the top, but do bear in mind the corporate ladder. Your circle of contacts will necessarily broaden as time goes on, networking is about knowing who is available to you first time round. Once you've done a certain amount of preparation you'll find yourself getting closer and closer to the people whom you think can really help you.

You must plan your approach to a very senior and influential person carefully. It is more than likely that none of them will be available the first time you call. You must realize the context in which you're working: people worth getting in touch with are very busy, and get networked all the time. Their acquaintance must be worked at and nurtured.

Cold-calling can be unnerving, but it is an approach you must be prepared to use to achieve career turnaround. Cold-calling may be used as something of a last resort, if there is no other way to approach someone and you don't know anyone who knows them. Cold-calling is more successful in some sectors than others — such as in financial services.

Cold-calling Techniques

The techniques of cold-calling include standing up while you make the call. This aids self-confidence. Choose a time when you feel positive and upbeat. The purpose of the call is to set up a meeting. Keep the conversation brief and give your 'victim' a choice of dates on which to meet up. Don't just offer to send a CV or samples of your work, and don't take no for an answer. Keep pressing. The trick is to make the people you are cold-calling feel that they might be passing up a valuable opportunity if they choose not to meet with you. If they will not agree to a meeting, try inviting them out to lunch. If they really seem determined to put you off, ring off and spend some more time thinking what might do the trick. Then call back a week or so later. They will be impressed at your persistence and determination, and you will get through in the end.

Making Initial Contact

How do you contact and get people to help you? Basically you've got to offer them a reason to want to help you. There's got to be something in it for them.

One of the ways to get people to want to help you is to be full of the latest information, so that they can learn interesting things from you. So be an interesting person — don't be dull and boring — be alive and upbeat, so they feel you're giving them something as well as taking. Say something that will arrest their attention: 'Well, I've been round this and I've talked to a number of people, and did you know that your competitors are doing this? And I've done a survey of this sector, and you might be interested to know that . . .' This sort of approach will get you noticed. You don't always need a contact to get a contact if you use new information judiciously. Information is key: use it to barter for help.

Being a Good Listener

Before you can help your helper, however, you have to learn the delicate art of communication, to know what to do when you talk to people. You can't be so introverted that you cannot speak. If this is the case you will need coaching on how to become more outgoing.

Nor do you want to be so extroverted that you dominate the conversation, because then you'll never learn what you wanted to find out in the first place. You've got to make it clear what it is you want to know, then sit back and really listen. A good listener will know when to delve further into an issue or when to ask for clarification of a point. You only learn from a conversation when you're listening; you never learn when you're doing all the talking.

When you react to what a person's said by trying to expand the point you feel he or she has made, then you're halfway to understanding the message being put across. If you're trying to clarify something, you're going to ask a question, and because you've made the question more specific you will get a better answer.

This is one of the ways you can impress people — you can ask smart perceptive, focused questions — not the blunderbuss query but the sharp rifle-shot one. You should also have back-up questions ready, just as the MPs do in the House of Commons. Have them ready, but don't be thinking of them all the time because then you'll miss the answer to your original question!

Of course you can't always know how people will react, but do try to identify with them: can you 'get inside' their heads and see yourself as they see you? Are you getting your message across? If not, what does this tell you about what you are doing right and what you are doing wrong?

Tips from a Salesperson

Have you the kind of flexible personality that enables you to appeal in the nicest possible way to quite a wide number of people? This an important attribute, and the one that good salespeople have, because when they go round and meet all their customers they are obviously going to have to appeal and get on with lots of different characters.

The best salespeople also remember things — their customers' birthdays, what they ordered last, what went wrong with a past order, their kids' names, when they've been ill, when the family's gone on holiday.

There are various ways of making people feel comfortable, and they're not all the same. When the salespeople we're talking about need to be brisk and ruthless they can be; and when they're with a customer who's more relaxed then they're relaxed. The successful salesperson not only needs to remember the type of person he or she is dealing with but also must be able to sense people's moods quickly. It is a question of knowing when to press ahead and when to withdraw, leaving the battle for another day. This can be particularly difficult to do over the telephone, without the help of body language. You need to cultivate your ability to pick up on very subtle nuances, and this takes a lot of experience.

Using a salesperson's tactics to network and sell yourself is crucial in the early stages of implementing career turnaround, when you're up against the very formidable task of convincing people that you really do want to achieve what you've set out to achieve.

Building Confidence

There are three stages to building self-confidence. The key point to remember is that confidence builds confidence, and to achieve career turnaround you are going to need confidence more than almost any other quality.

Stage one: desire — not ability — is the key factor that governs success. What holds many people back (in all walks of life but particularly in business) is that they think they haven't got what it takes. This should never be a factor, because it is desire and not ability that really counts. It is self-motivation that helps you become successful, not technical ability. Of course in an ideal world you'd want large measures of both basic ability and desire, yet many people have overcome limited ability by virtue of sheer motivation, while people with no desire but an abundance of ability have not always been successful.

Stage two: success breeds success. You cannot and almost certainly will not go through life with no troubles; there will always be setbacks. You can't always change your circumstances, but you can change your attitude. You must be able to think positively and overcome obstacles, to look ahead and be optimistic, to use success for more success.

Stage three: keep away from negative people. It is often the negative or fatalistic person who will hamper your motivation and undermine your confidence. Such people can hold you back, so try to avoid them, or maybe even infect them with your own enthusiasm and confidence. Of course there will always be days when you don't feel very good, successful or confident, but this is not the same as chronic persistent negativism, when you feel that nothing is possible. You must always believe that tomorrow is going to be better than today, and convey that feeling to all around you.

Getting Headhunted

Being approached and offered new career opportunities — even if you don't necessarily want them — shows that you might be ripe for a career turnaround. Being approached as a source of information is also significant; it shows that you have acquired valuable knowledge and authority in your field. All this can help you to make a career turnaround, if this is what you feel you'd like to do, or if you feel that it is a logical extension of what you've done already. For many people career turnaround is a continuing process, and once they have moved on from one thing to another, they may feel they want to move on again.

In any case, most of us like to keep in touch with any opportunities available in the marketplace. It's just one aspect of continually refining and improving upon your brand. People who are implementing career turnaround will also benefit from outside recognition of their achievements. For while it is very important to feel self-confident, it is also significant if the wider world — especially the very discerning and selective world of the headhunters — share your outlook.

Why should you go out of your way to cultivate headhunters? What is it like to be interviewed by them: how will they treat you? What kind of an impression would you like to make? Above all, how can you ensure that they will take you seriously?

Why the Headhunters Can Help You

Top headhunters are asked all the time to appraise people and compare them to their peers in the market. One of the best pieces of advice you can expect to get out of a headhunter is how you are rated in the market; this is generally a very intangible quantity, and something impossible to get an objective view on from any other source.

Very experienced headhunters can receive — often late in the evening — a 'fire brigade call' from a very senior executive, asking them to go down and see them immediately to answer their questions about the quality of their staff in relation to the rest of the marketplace. How would a headhunter rate their 30 most senior people? How good are they now, and are they likely to be able to stand up to competitive pressures to come? A good headhunter can offer an instant appraisal on the spot, giving an informed opinion on each case, taking into consideration where people have peaked and who, why and for what others would be interested in hiring them.

This is top-quality inside information. A good headhunter's appraisal will be analytical, unemotional and realistic, and will offer a completely new way of looking at a group of people. The headhunter is looking at his client's people in the context of the wider market in which they operate. Headhunters can see the big picture — this is one of the reasons why they can help you implement your career turnaround.

Being Interviewed by a Headhunter

A good headhunter will really make you feel that you've been put through an interview. You will realize straight away that he or she does this for a living. For their part headhunters know that any new person who crosses the threshold may provide them with new contacts, ideas and opportunities. You mustn't disappoint them.

As in the case of networking and acquiring a mentor, the person going to meet a headhunter — even for a very general, getting-to-know you meeting — needs to give as much as he or she gets. The more information you give a headhunter, the more you will get in return.

The headhunter may well manage to get you angry about things that you feel he or she doesn't know much about; this is a technique used to measure your response to issues close to your heart. How strongly do you feel about what you do? How motivated are you? What might you be prepared to sacrifice to get what you want?

You may find that the way in which headhunters ask questions is quite unlike anything you've come across before. When you actually analyse their questions later on you may realize they were not as probing as you'd thought; never the less headhunters are very good at eliciting information. The best ones use a lot of eye contact; they put their points over persuasively, and have a great deal of magnetism.

How Not to Impress a Headhunter

Making a good impression on a headhunter means, above all, having clarity of thought. You may be tempted to try and answer a question even if you don't know what you're talking about. Don't attempt it, it won't achieve anything. Some people feel a desperate urge to contribute to a conversation — even if they haven't been listening or thinking very carefully. These types of people will be seen, by the cognoscenti, as lightweights. You may come across as quite likeable, or even to have handled the interview well, but you will not appeal to a thinking person's headhunter. You may get away with a lot because of your enthusiasm and energy, but these traits, however positive, must be combined with a certain astuteness and sensitivity if you are to succeed.

Other people who will fail to impress are those who are somehow inadequate, who lack that killer instinct. Of course you don't want to put over the impression that you bite the heads off live chickens for breakfast, but you must be seen to have a motor in you, and as someone ready to take action if need be. You may be a very tender person, with a lot of skills. But whatever your position those working with you will get cross if you are seen to be ineffectual in any way.

If your idea of impressing a headhunter or a client is to be your usual low-key self, you won't even make an impact on people who are as low-key as you. And while it might be true that if they only got through that low-key exterior they'd find you very bright and eager — *they might never bother to try*. You've got to impress them straight away, you've got to be assertive and take initiative.

How to Attract a Headhunter

Attracting headhunters means polishing your image constantly and keeping up your appeal. You must work at enhancing the brand you have created. Basic advice on how to get headhunted will always include standard points on CV writing. Some less well-quoted tips for attracting the headhunters include:

- Think of yourself in terms of sales and marketing
- Analyse your skills and pay attention to your presentation
- Get to know how executive search works, looking out for search firms that deal particularly with your field of endeavour
- Send in a brief, factual, specific and up-to-date CV, which includes details of your current salary and expectations for your future

- Ask an influential friend to recommend you to a headhunter
- Become more visible in your company/industry
- Acquire further qualifications and skills — you'll gain new contacts in the process
- Join the relevant trade associations, perhaps gaining an office in or being elected to its committee
- Get noticed publicly: Write articles for industry/general publications; write letters to the press; or get yourself into your company brochure/report and accounts.

The Phone Call

- Be businesslike and professional
- Identify whom you are talking to: how prestigious is the search firm, and how senior is the headhunter?
- Never ask how the headhunter came across your name; try to give the impression that you are accustomed to and familiar with being headhunted
- Never give away confidential information: Be discreet!
- Try not to come across as too aloof or hard-to-get — you will sound over-confident and brash
- Listen carefully; don't talk too much
- Ask specific questions about the opportunities on offer, but don't expect to find out all the details at this stage
- Ascertain which qualifications are required, and the level of the job
- Try to find out why an external search is being made
- Is the headhunter's client well-established or is it a new business?
- Is the client expanding, stabilizing or restructuring?
- Will the headhunter give an indication of the salary on offer?
- Use this telephone call to get you to the next stage: the interview.

The Interview

- First impressions count — You won't get a second chance
- Dress and behave as the epitome of the professional
- Look tasteful but with a hint of individuality

- Never lie about anything, especially your salary
- Emphasize the strong, positive reasons for any changes in your career
- Don't try to sell yourself too strongly
- Don't come across as desperate — even if you are currently unemployed, give the impression that you have several irons in the fire
- Let the consultant try to sell the job to you rather than the other way round
- Be circumspect but not off-hand; ask relevant questions
- Be personable and try to show you have a range of interests — bring photocopies of relevant published articles or studies, and try to convey your knowledge of the market and your place in it
- When you feel that all relevant questions have been asked and answered, politely break off, as work is pressing; thank the consultant for the chance to discuss the opportunity
- Be aware that the competition for the opportunity will be tough
- Prepare yourself for a meeting with the client — be entirely frank about other positions you're being considered for.

All of these tips apply just as well to approaching senior executives who are looking to hire new management or when you are dealing with anyone in a position to help you with your career turnaround.

Feedback/Control

Go back to the plan and objectives you created for yourself. In the light of the implementation schemes set out in this chapter you may want to revise your plans — perhaps you've realized that you'll need more time, or better networking. Change it as you wish; do whatever it takes so that you can implement your plan now.

This re-evaluation process should be continual. Just as corporations execute regular feedback and control services, you too should review your situation on a steady basis. Refer to changes in the marketplace and within your own personal and work life; as your objectives take shape they will alter as a matter of course. Accept this and you can work with change to your benefit. Feedback will be available from many quarters, professional and private. Without it your objectives risk becoming static and less and less grounded in the present. Any strategy needs to evolve, adjusting to any errors you might have made or changes in your circumstance for good or ill.

With these supplies under your belt you will be well on your way to achieving career turnaround and making sure it is a lasting one.

Part Three

Case Studies

This book has examined a 'critical path' or strategy for individuals to achieve dramatic change in their careers, based on elements pursued in corporate turnarounds.

We have looked at features of successful companies — especially in terms of clear objectives, thorough SWOT analysis and auditing, in careful and detailed market research, in strong product development and branding, in the determined implementation of a well-thought-out strategic plan, and in subsequent feedback and control — all the elements of a well-performing company, which can be closely translated to peoples' careers.

Now we will examine thirteen case studies in detail. There are several aspects that many company turnarounds have in common with career turnarounds, as will be seen in these case studies. As companies move out of the public sector into private hands, as they spin-off individual parts as entrepreneurial start-ups, originating from big corporates, as small enterprises grow into big concerns, as companies change their products and activities, adding some and taking away others, as they adapt their functions from manufacturing to marketing or from doing to advising — so people change their careers. These case studies include examples of:

- staying in the same field but writing about rather than doing it

- staying with the same public sector while altering one's activities (teaching to preaching)

- moving from the public sector — in the diplomatic corps — to the private one — banking
- starting from nothing to form one's own company
- turning a hobby into a business
- moving from a big corporate to a small start-up in a new field
- moving from a big financial corporate to one's own consulting business

These career turnarounds have been achieved by people from a variety of backgrounds and experiences. Which ones do you find yourself identifying with? Could you achieve what they have achieved? No? Then your way ahead is clear. Is there anything stopping *you from doing this, or achieving any of the other career turnarounds described here?*

Arnab Banerji: Eye Surgeon/Investment Banker

'My career turnaround was imposed upon me because of a car accident. I received a head injury, and as a result developed a squint for several years, and so I couldn't get my insurance to go on operating. I had always wanted to be a surgeon, and I was angry, furious, even devastated that I couldn't go on being one. All my family and my then girlfriend had a very hard time. I discharged myself early from hospital and decided I was going to recover fast. I threw out anybody who came to visit me. However, I now have an enjoyable and successful career in the City, although the transition was difficult at times.'

Background

'I had been born in India, in Agra, and came to the UK when I was three years old. I had always wanted to be a doctor, although when I was younger I was interested in being an astronomer and then a physicist. I was influenced to become a doctor by an older relative, who studied bones, which seemed to be all around the place when I was growing up. I was doing quite well in my medical career — as a medical graduate I had good prospects; I passed my exams and I was working at a hospital in Oxford at the time of the accident.

'I was very happy being a surgeon, and I wanted to go on to be a consultant. I was then 27. In March 1983, I decided to leave medicine, and was faced with the prospect of launching myself into a whole new career. What was I going to do about this?

'At first I still clung to the hope of being an eye surgeon, until a friend of mine at Moorfields told me categorically that I just couldn't be one any more. What I had liked about eye surgery was that it is very precise and neat, and in a way it's a combination of medicine and surgery. Eyes are windows to the soul, literally. In them you can see diseases, from the mundane to the exotic, and you can see the immediate consequences of your surgical handiwork.'

Influences and Mentors

'When faced with having to choose a new career, I remembered that some of my brightest friends in my peer group at University had gone into the City. I had respected this decision at the time, and now thought that this sounded an exciting way of life. I didn't understand anything about the City then, and when I first became a surgeon it was not as attractive and fashionable as it later became. So in thinking of going into the City in the early- to mid-1980s, my timing was quite good.

'I went to see the Dean of the Medical School at Oxford for help in considering my new career options. He came from a business background — his family were related to the Vestey's — and he believed that people could do whatever they wanted. He played a great part in helping me decide what I wanted to do. A medical training is quite narrow: I didn't really know anything about any other occupation. He recommended strongly that I should go into the City. He said that I should give it two years and if I was very miserable, I could do something else.

'My old tutor at college was also significant as a mentor. He said I should try the City for two or three years. He also pointed out that it was a good time for me to try a new career: I was not married, and I was still young.

'I also sounded various other people out about my new proposed career. The doctors and consultants thought I was mad, they said I could have gone into general practice, that I didn't necessarily have to leave the medical profession. But when I couldn't become an ophthalmic consultant, I immaturely thought that anything else would be second rate.

'Luckily, my father was also a great support to me. He had already had a number of different careers himself. He ran the family business, an Indian restaurant, and also had an import/export business in

Berlin. In his time, he had been a pilot, a schoolteacher and a chemist before setting up his own business. He too encouraged me to go into the City. This helped convince me, especially because the Dean and my tutor at college had said the same thing.'

Achieving Career Turnaround

'How did I go about trying to get a job in the City? First of all, I undertook a commissioned research project on behalf of a bank, looking at a hospital contract in the Third World and doing an inventory analysis. A friend of mine in the City had given me this work. Then I applied to a number of merchant banks: I hadn't then heard of stockbroking. I went in on the "milk round" (yearly recruitment drive by City firms) and had four offers of jobs: one from Schroders, one each from Chase Manhattan and another American house, and one from Kleinwort Benson. I was most interested in the British houses, as I felt I knew a bit about them. In the end I chose Schroders, as I actually knew some people there.

'I felt I was very lucky to get these job offers, and with great initial enthusiasm I joined as a trainee. I was there for three and a half years, and they treated me very well. I left after this time, as I was headhunted to join Nomura, and was offered a great deal of money. Schroders generally paid modestly, although their stars were well rewarded. Nomura offered me more than three times what I had been making. I didn't really want to move, so when they asked me what I would take to leave, I made up a number and I was amazed when they agreed. They were then an unknown quantity in the City but obviously fated to do well. I liked it there, but I was offered the job as head of Research at a division of Citicorp, so I went there in June 1989. Looking back, I went to Nomura for the money, but found it was a great place to work. I went to Citicorp for the prospect of greater responsibility.'

Changes and Contrasts

'If I think about it, there were unsatisfactory aspects of my previous job as a surgeon, even though I was generally very happy in this role. For a start, the hours were very long, although in medicine you tend to expect this, and you don't know any different. I wasn't bothered by the lack of money, as I had no time to spend any. I did resent some rather unfair bosses in medicine who could easily destroy people's careers if they took a strong dislike to them. This doesn't happen in the City — if you have ability it will be recognized outside as well as inside.

'There are some similarities between the two jobs. In the City, one of the important things is getting on with clients. In medical life, you also have to get on with people. There were some who criticized me for going into what was perceived as a less "valuable" career. Certainly there are aspects that I miss about my old life, such as the simple thing of helping people. It's interesting too that now, when I say I am an investment banker, people see me as clever and sharp, whereas medics are seen as clever and nice.

'In general, the trust, acceptance and respect you can instantly earn is much higher as a doctor. In all communities, among all classes and races, doctors are highly regarded. As a doctor, I could meet someone and gain their immediate trust. I could also meet top people and be accepted instantly. But as an investment banker, people think that you are a sharp so-and-so, bright but not necessarily that honest.'

Reviewing the Situation

'In considering my career turnaround, I didn't really analyse my strengths and weaknesses, and whether or not I could work in the City. I just assumed that I could, if I tried hard enough. But I was very unhappy my first year in the City, and I felt that I had made a big mistake. I missed medicine desperately.

'Also, I had made the transition from being quite important and authoritative, to being somebody who was very junior. I had taken very important decisions before, in matters of life and death, but now I was being treated the same as any trainee.

'I also felt the lack of money, paradoxically. In medicine you work long hours and live in hospital accommodation and, as I said, have relatively few opportunities to spend money. There were few opportunities to spend money, so you didn't really think about it, and your lifestyle tended to be fairly modest.

'When I went into the City, I felt this lack of money, especially because I had to find and pay for my own accommodation. I had few friends and I didn't like having to commute long distances all the time. I doubted the wisdom of my choice to go into the City frequently, but was determined to stick it out for two years. At the end of these two years I was doing rather well, so I decided to stay.

'I sat and passed the necessary exams I needed to take, and just before I left Schroders, I sat a series of examinations in the US to see if I still knew anything about medicine. These exams were entirely voluntary and qualified me to work as a medic in the US. I haven't needed to use them, but I still wanted the challenge and I was still interested in medicine, in spite of everything.

'By the time I was headhunted to Nomura, I had come to stop missing medicine quite so much. It is now six or seven years since I last operated on an eye. Being at Nomura was very different, there was more cut and thrust, and now Citicorp is another culture altogether. It was quite sociable at Nomura, as people went out together and drank together more, but then they squabbled together more. At Schroders, it was more collegiate, but people did not socialize so much. In a Japanese house such as Nomura there tends to be quite a family atmosphere, which is something the Japanese encourage.

'Would I consider another career? Possibly, as I am quite interested in the idea of working for myself, or working for a charity, helping animals, old people or trying to solve Third World problems. But there is no reason for me to do any of these at the moment, as it seems I am being groomed for interesting things at Citicorp. Here, it is a very open and democratic atmosphere, with a big mixture of nationalities. There is a feeling that the sky's the limit.'

Practical Advice

'In offering advice to others contemplating career turnaround, I would emphasize that there is a cost to achieving change. You mustn't go to something new just because you think the grass is greener, and you mustn't run away from something, or you will be going from one unhappiness to another.

'You have to be prepared to give up preconceived views and challenge the views of others. I do not think that the City is dishonest. I have an answer for those who suggest that it is just moving money around, without creating wealth. Now I look down on people who have such criticisms of the City; they just don't understand. It is important to be able to justify your new role to yourself and others. I now really believe that the City does make a contribution different from but perhaps as important as that of the NHS.'

Dick Francis: Jockey/Novelist

'I was a champion jockey, and after I retired, I turned to novel-writing, and I have now written 29 novels, including some which have been made into films. Inevitably, all jockeys have to give up the racecourse at some point: it's a young man's game. But not all of us jockeys have been able to make the transition to a completely new career, one which has not been an anti-climax. I now enjoy my career as a novelist very much, and it pays much more than I ever earned as a jockey. I'm now based in Florida, and will probably continue staying here most of the time.'

Background

'The reason why I decided to retire from being a jockey, at the time when I did, is fairly unusual. Of course, I knew I would have to pack up at some point, but what happened was this: I was riding the Queen Mother's horse at the 1956 Grand National. My horse was 10 lengths in front, and we had only 25 yards to go; but it collapsed on me.

'I had had a series of nasty falls that season, and I was finding that it was taking me longer to recover than before. Most steeplechase jockeys give up in their early 30s. I felt that this would be a good time to get out. I had made my mark in the leading jockey's championships. I was 36.

'Before I announced my retirement I had gained an introduction to the man who was going to be my future literary agent, John Johnson. He had encouraged me to start writing my autobiography, and I began this in the summer of 1956. By January 1957 it was half-written.

'When I retired from the racecourse, I was asked out to lunch by the sports editor of the *Sunday Express*, Bill Smith. He was interested in the fact that I had half-written my autobiography, and he seemed to think that I had the potential to write. He asked me if I would write articles for the *Sunday Express* on the current racing scene. I said that I would; this led to 16 years of employment with the *Sunday Express*.

'I started writing novels in late 1960. My wife had pointed out that I had two sons to educate, and even though my income as a newspaper columnist wasn't bad, I had suffered a decline in income after giving up being a jockey.

'So I wrote my first novel. My autobiography had been published in 1957, in the beginning of December. It did so well that it had been reprinted before Christmas, and is still in print today. The publishers Michael Joseph, who published my autobiography, had included in their contract a clause that if I wrote anything else they would like to consider it. So my agent, John Johnson, took my next manuscript to them in the Autumn of 1961. This was *Dead Cert*.

'I didn't start another novel until after *Dead Cert* had come out six months later, because I wanted to know how it would be received. It did quite well, so then I started on my next novel, which was published in 1964. This was *Nerve*.'

Choices

'I did consider the possibility of other jobs after I gave up being a jockey. I was offered a job judging on racecourses, but the Jockey Club said that either I must become a full-time judge or stay a full-time newspaper man, and I couldn't do both. I realized that being a newspaper man was better paid, and I continued writing for the *Sunday Express* until 1973.

'I do miss my life as a jockey. For ten years after I retired, I constantly missed the competition and the joy of riding good horses. I still occasionally ride, but of course it is not the same.'

Influences and Mentors

'I have never had any training in writing. The most I have done is to write letters to England from Africa during the Second World War. But my wife, who had a university education, has always been a great help to me. She never doubted that I could become a novelist, and she was very good at convincing others too. She has been a constant source of encouragement and inspiration.

'So, in my career turnaround, my wife played a very important part, together with John Johnson, my literary agent. Sadly, Johnson is now dead; my agent is now Andrew Hewson, John's former partner and manager of John Johnson (Authors' Agents) Ltd.

'Michael Joseph himself was also a strong influence. I knew him when I was a jockey and rode for him on occasion. He was very sympathetic towards my efforts to write my autobiography and my first novel. When Michael Joseph died, his widow took over the task of acting as my editor and running the business.'

The Challenge of a New Career

'To be successful as a novelist, I feel that you have got to get your facts right and do your research. I have concentrated on writing about the world of horses and I research very carefully the aspects of my novels which I don't know much about. I once did a book about wines, *Proof*, which I researched very thoroughly. I also did a book about the staging of the Moscow Olympics (*Slay-Ride*), and another about photography (*Reflex*). Each of these involved a great deal of in-depth research work.

'Also, I feel that another important thing is to tell a story without using surplus words, and to get the reader to want to turn the page, to have to go on and finish reading.

'I keep looking forwards to the future, trying to achieve better work. I am sensitive to the competition, and I constantly try to make my current manuscript better than my previous ones. I keep writing, seeing it as a constant challenge, even though I'm now 70. My 29th novel came out recently [September 1990] — which is also set with a racing background.

'My writing skills came fairly early on in my career as a novelist, and I find that I don't have to change very much of what I write. From page 1 to page 360 I rarely change anything. I write it all out in longhand in a notebook, and I do all my own typing on a word processor. The best thing about word processors are that they are quieter than typewriters. My wife has always been my greatest editor; if I can get work past her, then I can get it past anyone.'

Changes and Contrasts

'In my career as a writer, I have travelled a great deal, much more so than I did as a jockey. Sometimes I am asked to give lectures and public presentations on the subjects of my novels. I moved to Ocean Boulevard in Florida in the US, initially just to carry out research about the auctioning of horses for one of my novels, *Knock Down*. I enjoyed it here so much, that I decided to stay. Also, my wife gets asthma when the weather is damp, so we thought we would be better off living in a warm climate.

'Inevitably, my lifestyle and habits have changed since I gave up being a jockey, but I still get up early. I still feel I have to be out of the house by about 6:30 a.m. So I tend to go for a long walk by the ocean and then have a swim. I don't do any riding any more, except when I am back in England.

'My life was very active as a jockey and now it is less so. However, I find writing harder work than the physical demands of being a jockey and riding in top competitions. I go to the races quite a lot, and I always go to the Grand National, where I am a trustee of the Grand National Aintree Fund. Often, Michael Joseph sponsor races at the other racecourses, chiefly Plumpton in Sussex, where the races they sponsor are always named after my most recent books. I go racing occasionally in the States.

'Other jockeys have done interesting things after they gave up the racecourse; both John Francome and Brough Scott have also written books, and the latter has written for *The Sunday Times*. But they have not been as successful as I have, in terms of their output. Being a novelist has enabled me to continue to be well-known, successful and prosperous in what I do.

'I would not really consider attempting career turnaround again. I am not really interested now in being anything but a novelist. I did nearly get involved in films once, when *Dead Cert* was being made into a film. I was present during some of the production, but I felt it was ruined on the cutting room floor. However, it all helps to sell books, and the more books I can sell the better.

'*The Racing Game*, a British television series which ran for six episodes, was based on my novel *Odds Against*, and in the US, the Dick Francis mystery series, all based on my stories, continues to be shown all around the country.'

Margaret Haas: Wall Street Broker/ Recruitment Consultant for Japanese Candidates

'My international executive recruiting company, Haas & McBryde International, is now over five years old. We work exclusively between the West and Japan in cross-cultural recruiting. We have an office in Tokyo as well as an office here in New York. Most of our work is done in Japan, introducing Japanese men and women to Western corporations.

'I had been on Wall Street for seven years, working with American corporations selling financial products. I ended up by selling Japanese stocks to American institutional investors for Merrill Lynch — that was my last 'proper' job. I never really enjoyed selling financial products, but I'm now very happy inventing and building my own career.'

Background

'After studying at Harvard Graduate School in East Asian Studies and spending three years in Japan I wanted to use my hard-earned Japanese language skills and understanding of the Japanese culture. At that time many of the large banks were looking for Americans with international experience, and Chemical Bank offered me a job with their Asia Group. On Wall Street, I often found myself casually "interviewing" my peers and my seniors, asking them why they were doing what they were doing. I have always been fascinated by why people choose the careers that they do, what motivates them to work in their chosen fields.

'The story behind why I got involved in recruiting, and in making such a big career change, goes back to when I first visited Japan as a student in 1969. Japan is poor in natural resources, so the Japanese see people as their major national asset. The Japanese initiate, value and nourish personal and business friendships over time and in ways uncommon in the West. The Japanese are tremendous networkers, and the role of go-between is built into the culture. I realized that I enjoyed networking, and it is easier to do this in homogeneous Japan, much easier than in heterogeneous America, where the giving of favours is less predictably connected with the receipt of them. I have a number of Japanese friends because I've been involved now in Japan for 21 years — half my life.

'I never saw myself as properly suited for Wall Street, and I found that outlets for my love of networking and putting people together were limited. Wall Street was transactional, not people-orientated. Yet I had been on Wall Street for seven years, working with four different American financial institutions. After lending to Japanese financial institutions with Chemical Bank for three years, I became an institutional stockbroker. I taught American retail brokers how to sell Japanese stocks, then I sold American stocks to Japanese financial institutions. Finally, at Merrill Lynch, I sold Japanese stocks to American institutional investors.

'But if I didn't want to sell financial products, where did I belong? I began to take motivational workshops at weekends, and I learned that I had to take responsibility for the quality of my life. I was 37 and I felt dissatisfied; I wanted to do something different. I began to see executive recruiting as a way of combining my interests in deal-making and counselling. Being a stockbroker had taught me the basics of negotiating and closing a deal, and with some trepidation I made two successful placements on my own to supplement my income during my last two years on Wall Street. But I was doubtful for a while as to whether I had the skills and the interest for headhunting.'

Taking the Plunge

'I finally left Wall Street after one fateful meeting with a respected friend in which I realized, with a new-found clarity, that I was continuing to sell stocks merely to stay involved with Japan!

'Following my resignation from Merrill Lynch, I explored both consulting and executive recruiting. The one lesson my brokerage career taught me was that you make money by making offers and requests and obtaining and fulfilling promises. My job was to put the best buyer with the best seller, and facilitate the deal. I began calling British financial firms in New York who had called me at Merrill Lynch when they were looking for Japanese-speaking brokers. Three weeks later I came close to closing my first deal, which would have earned me one-third of what my annual salary had been at Merrill Lynch. The candidate declined the offer, but I acquired a passion for recruiting! My efforts became Haas & McBryde International.

'You may ask how I raised the money to set up my company, and if I needed much to start with, but the answer is I didn't. The timing was very lucky. Unwittingly, I started up in the middle of a worldwide bull market. I had a number of clients who gave me recruiting assignments, with the idea that if I didn't succeed they would hire me to sell Japanese stocks again. On their behalf I searched for international brokers, traders and research analysts, particularly those who were bilingual in English and Japanese. I also received a small consulting contract from business friends at the Mitsubishi Corporation, which effectively covered my rent for a year. This contract somewhat mysteriously started soon after I left Merrill Lynch and ended without explanation once my business was on a sound footing. As a result, I discovered I had a safety net.'

Influences

'I started this business working from my apartment at first, and one thing led to another. My partner, Marnie McBryde, was then working as a career counsellor for international and domestic MBA [Master of Business Administration] students at New York University. She had counselled me in getting out of the stockbroking business. We began working together informally at first: I would describe assignments and she would provide the names of candidates.

'She taught me a great deal about counselling candidates, making recruiting even more attractive. I had said to her, "If I start this recruiting company and it survives, are you interested?" She had said she would be but wanted to wait and see how it went for a little while, saying "let me see, let me think about it." But before I had even got my first placement she quit NYU and joined me full time.'

The Challenges of a New Career

'Our first really big client on retainer was Citicorp, and they sent us to Tokyo and asked us to recruit for their Tokyo office, as they wanted Japanese employees. The financial markets in New York were booming, but in Tokyo it was like finding ourselves in the middle of a gold rush! When Japanese clients in Kabuto-cho (Tokyo's equivalent of Wall Street) had told me two years before that Tokyo would form the third point of a triangle with London and New York, I had been sceptical. Two years later, every foreign institution wanted an office in Tokyo, and they were desperate for bilingual Japanese or anyone who could help them get set up.

'Seventy per cent of our business in the past three years has been for non-Japanese companies in Tokyo, recruiting Japanese men and women. Most of our placements are bilingual Japanese, not Westerners. The remainder of our work is recruiting Japanese people for American firms in the United States. Occasionally we recruit for Japanese companies, but this is not a large part of our business. I would like to do more of this recruiting, but Japanese companies are not so easy to recruit for. The idea of executive recruiting is still fairly new to the Japanese.

'When I started my business in 1985, only a few of the major foreign-owned recruiting firms had offices in Tokyo, and they didn't all understand the financial markets. Local Japanese recruiting firms did not understand recruiting, and had to overcome the surprise and even horror that Japanese were now trying to make money in the traditional non-monetary role of go-between.

'The Japanese I'm looking for don't necessarily have to speak English. I speak Japanese fluently so I can interview them and I can place them with Japanese who don't speak English. If they're working for a Western company, the Western company usually wants them to be able to speak English, but some of the American companies are desperate enough or big enough not to need this. The Management Information Systems group, for example, might be run by a bilingual head with staff below him or her that speak only Japanese. So we do some of that, although not very much. As the business has grown, my most challenging assignments have been searching for Japanese to be top executives and company presidents.'

Changes and Contrasts

'When I was on Wall Street, I was selling Japanese financial products but I didn't feel that close to the Japanese. I didn't need my Japanese language that much. I wanted to deal with people, not stocks. When you actually succeed in placing someone it's so satisfying, both in terms of the client and the candidate. You get very close to them in the process. I could never really get this sort of closeness to people in my Wall Street days. And I didn't get to travel very much, but was more or less chained to the desk. Now I go to Tokyo about every six weeks for two or three weeks. My partner and I alternate, or occasionally we go together.

'I did well financially at Chemical and at Merrill, but my business is pretty profitable now. I never really had to make that much of a financial sacrifice to make the break and set up my own business. Even though we're a relatively small operation, the clients are so desperate for people, and we seem to have a knack for it, that we now have a tremendous network of clients. I think the Japanese love being headhunted — they get a bit of a buzz out of it — they're really curious. Honestly, I think they find it a special treat to be called from New York and then to be met by foreign women who already know all about them. The final surprise is when they discover I speak Japanese as well!

'It's a funny business, working between New York and Tokyo. With the kind of travel that we do and the fact that ours is truly an international business, in some ways I work much harder than I ever did in my previous career — but I enjoy it much more now. The great thing is the freedom of working for yourself, compared with the work I was doing before. Of course there are special problems in running a business from two different centres. It can be crazy-making — and I mean constantly. I think the hardest thing is not being in Tokyo or being in New York, not being in either place for long enough to have a 'normal' life. My life is very hectic.

'We work from a lovely old brownstone building, more like a home than an office, which is another great contrast from working on Wall Street. We have a garden in the back and we say "We know it's not a typical business address, but can we offer you a beer in the garden?" Another fun aspect of doing what I'm doing now is that, on Wall Street, in Chemical Bank or Merrill Lynch, I was one of hundreds, thousands, selling stocks. Now there aren't that many people doing what I'm doing, in fact there's no one who's doing exactly what we are.

'I am thrilled by the way I have been able to turn my life and my career around, and to have the two mesh together in such a productive and satisfying way. I still ask everyone I meet why they have the careers they have, and if they're not happy, I like to help them find the satisfaction that I have found in my new career.'

Michael Harrison: Managing Director of Multinational Subsidiaries/ Antique Dealer

'I'm now an antiques dealer, working on my own account, dealing through a shop which I've bought, handling valuations for insurance and probate. I worked at an auctioneering house to gain practical experience before I felt able to branch out on my own. This all seems a far cry from my original job at Beecham, where I was a director of a subsidiary and responsible for developing a number of Beecham's subsidiaries overseas, before being made redundant.'

Background

'There were a great many Beecham subsidiaries all round the world, and five years ago they were having a very difficult time. The entire company was facing unprecedented problems. I found myself one of perhaps two thousand members of staff — a fair proportion of the whole — who were being made redundant. Two thousand is a guess: the figures were never published.

'These layoffs were part of the rescue management strategy that was being implemented at that time. Previously, Beecham had acquired very many brands around the world (*Bovril* and *Marmite*, for example), and it was decided to get rid of many of these. They had looked good in the sales figures and on the balance sheet, and Beecham had got some growth out of them, but the company as a whole was going off on tangents, in too many different directions at the same time. I watched the management literally going to pieces, with senior managers bent on protecting their own — not surprising in the circumstances.

'I was made redundant in 1985. I was one of the first to go and it took me by surprise, especially as my businesses had just put in large profit increases. I knew that things were getting difficult, but I didn't realize that redundancies would be implemented so rapidly, and all across the board like they were. But when a company is getting rid of people, it has to take a broad view.

'My career turnaround all began when I was called into the personnel department. I thought it was to discuss salaries in the overseas subsidiaries. But it soon dawned on me that I was being informed that I was to be made redundant. It was all quite stunning; nothing like this had ever happened to me before.

'It didn't seem that much of a comfort at the time, but I was offered outplacement services paid for by Beecham. I went to see Pauline Hyde at her offices in Lincoln's Inn Fields. Her firm was very helpful, especially in helping me keep my self-esteem and get over the trauma of being made redundant. I was given a small pension by Beecham, and experienced an initial three weeks of consultation and advice at Pauline Hyde's and access to my counsellor thereafter.'

Considering Career Turnaround

'In considering what else I could do in terms of my next job, I felt that really I had done my stint in industry, and if I was honest with myself I was fairly fed up with it. Also I was 50 years old, and I felt that although there was a chance that an executive of 50 might get another job, I reckoned that it was unlikely to be of the same status and rank as the one I had left.

'I was informed that Pauline Hyde maintains that over 60 per cent of the people going through her hands at her outplacement firm end up with a better job than the one they were sacked from. I wasn't that convinced, though: I felt that these statistics were more true of people younger than myself.'

Choices

'I knew I was at the peak of my business career when I left Beecham. I'd achieved what I had wanted to achieve, and I felt quite assured that

I didn't need to prove anything else. I felt like using this opportunity to do something completely different, and the consultant provided by Pauline Hyde encouraged me to do this.

'We spent a lot of time discussing my very long-established hobby in the antique world, in collecting and restoring antique furniture. This hobby had begun when I was aged 13, and I had never lost interest in it despite my travels and commitments at Beecham. I had sometimes thought about making it my principal activity, yet there had always been a Catch-22: if I left Beecham without a pension, it would have been very difficult to set up in the antiques business without any initial financing, yet whilst I was still at Beecham I obviously had no time to do anything about it. It would have been hard to leave Beecham before this because I couldn't have obtained a good financial deal if I'd left at my own instigation.

'Through the help of Pauline Hyde's consultants, I wrote four letters to the four major auctioneering houses in London, at this stage simply inquiring as to whether or not they had any vacancies. As a result I had four interviews. In retrospect I was lucky, and also I had picked a good moment, although I wasn't necessarily aware of this at the time. I soon heard back that Bonham's — one of the most prestigious auctioneering houses in London — actually did have a vacancy, and in addition I had letters expressing real interest from two other houses.'

The Benefit of Experience

'I accepted the offer from Bonham's, and they made me their Head of Valuations. I soon discovered that my basic business skills, which I'd rather taken for granted, having acquired them almost subconsciously during my years at Beecham, were now in great demand. Beecham is known for its very strong administration practices and attention to administrative detail, and the skills I'd picked up there were highly valued in my new role in the auction business.

'I was quite shocked at the comparatively sloppy business practice going on in the department. One of their worst problems was their tendency to keep their records imperfectly. I could hardly believe this when I first came across it, but Bonham's would do valuations without presenting invoices. Even where these went out the department would fail to check up on debtors. They were generally fairly disorganized. One of my first achievements there, which wasn't that difficult but made a lot of difference, was improving their receivables situation by setting up a chasing system for collecting debts effectively.

'Many other improvements which Bonham's could make to their business soon became obvious to me. It was remarkable to me that Bonham's had neglected to take full advantage of the fact that solicitors are one of the main sources of obtaining valuation business, as a result of their probate work. I explained to Bonham's that if we could show our solicitor clients that we could take much of the administrative work off their hands, then clearly we could attract more business through this source. The success of my "tracking system" with solicitors was shown by the fact that my ideas were rapidly copied by our competitors.'

Learning New Skills

'The new skills I required for working for Bonham's were partly related to the business skills I had already learned at Beecham as well as the skills I had acquired through being an antiques collector for so many years. There were however significant new skills and abilities I had to learn. For example, although I had an academic knowledge of antique objects, I was not so good at pricing. This hadn't been so important to me in fields where I was active as a collector. In my hobby I had collected mainly walnut furniture dating from 1680 to 1740. I now had to learn about prices for all other periods; but I enjoyed this and it wasn't difficult.'

Changes and Contrasts

'I did make some financial sacrifices to achieve career turnaround, but I had my pension from Beecham, which meant that I did have a basic income anyway. The auction business as a rule is not well paid; people in this line of work don't tend to do it for the money. It struck me that many of the specialists in the auction business would be totally unemployable in any other capacity, and thus do not necessarily command large emoluments.

'There are certain aspects of my former role that I do miss. When I was at Beecham, I enjoyed getting on an aeroplane and travelling to overseas subsidiaries, where I was free to find and apply solutions to their problems. I particularly liked operating out of the reach of the head office, especially as Beecham got into more and more trouble and head office became an increasingly unattractive place to be. When I was travelling overseas I took decisions on the spot, off my own bat. I was fairly confident about doing this, although I was relieved when they turned out well. I miss this decision-making responsibility.

'Also, I still have friends at Beecham, and in some ways I miss working with them, but I don't miss the work there generally very much now. In my new career I feel fulfilled, relaxed and no longer concerned with the competitive edge of developing a multinational enterprise, nor with the ins and outs of office politics.'

'One of the problems in the early days at Bonham's was caused by the fact that many of the management team there weren't prepared to acknowledge that I knew as much as I did. They saw me as a "new boy," which of course in some ways I was. Yet in fact I knew a lot more than they did in some fields, which is understandable because I was older, with nearly 40 years of collecting and decades of sound business experience in a big multinational corporation.

'Looking at my skills as a whole, going into the antiques business was the best thing I could have done. I did think about other options: I could have become a business consultant, or I could have gone into various subsidiaries of a large business and helped turn them around. I did look at other job opportunities, but I didn't really fancy them. The job at Bonham's suited me very well indeed, in terms of my skills and inclination.'

Achieving Career Turnaround

'In terms of the timing involved, I was made redundant and left Beecham in May 1985; I spent in all six weeks receiving counselling at Pauline Hyde's; and I was offered my job at Bonham's in June 1985. I worked at Bonham's for one and a half years before setting up on my own, and have been working for myself since early 1987. I now concentrate on dealing and the restoration of antique furniture. I'm a careful restorer and I get good results.

'At first, I decided I didn't want the burden and responsibility of maintaining retail premises, but I met a young unemployed man who had trained in retailing and wanted to run a shop. I put up the capital and he ran the shop. It seemed a very good idea at the time. I talked to him about antiques and restoration, trying to teach him something about the business. I did the buying and the restoring, and planned that in seven or eight years I would hand everything over to him.

'However, things didn't work out exactly as I had planned, as he felt that this rate of growth was too slow, and he became dissatisfied. I bought him out, and now my shop is run by two women, one of whom was formerly a demonstrator in the Harrods perfume department and the other a senior secretary. They are both very able and do a good selling job.

'With my background at Beecham, my shop, although it is a very small-scale business, is run according to sophisticated management accounting practices, assessing my monthly cash-flow and profit and loss. My experience of being in a large multinational is not inappropriate even in the context of a small shop. It's still a business, and should be run like one.

'In theory I would be prepared to learn a new business and undertake another career turnaround. I did have a friend who ran a company distributing custom-made waste-paper baskets to hotel chains. I was interested in this and thought about joining him. But on balance I am very glad I chose what I'm doing now.'

Pauline Hyde: Housewife/ Outplacement Consultant

'Initially I didn't have much of a career: My husband and I ran a small company and I was director. But when I did embark on a career, I first worked in a firm of a management consultants, then as a partner in a design company, and ultimately started my own outplacement company. This was one of the earliest firms of its kind in London, and the first to be set up and run by a woman.'

Background

'My career turnaround was due not to just one factor, but was a progress thing. Initially it was forced upon me, rather than being something I planned. I was an only child and rather unaware of how businesses were run. When my first marriage came to an end and I didn't have any children, I was free to do something with my life, a need which I hadn't recognized before.

'With luck I was able to get hired by a small firm of management consultants, as subsidiary of Binder Hamlyn the charter accountants. At that time the firm was called MWM (London) Ltd; subsequently the name was changed to Binder Hamlyn Fry & Co. Ltd.

'It wasn't easy being a woman executive in the City in the 1950s. We were in a very small minority — many of the partners' secretaries were men.'

Influences and Mentors

'I was extremely lucky in that I worked with some excellent people who have had a great influence on my life. Bob Fry was a particularly enlightened guru figure, and was most influential. I got on very well with him, and learned a lot. I was also greatly influenced by Fred Oldfield, a psychologist who taught me about psychometric assessment. Through him I realized the value of my skills, and he helped me to develop these further. I had a good ability to write, and I was good at recruiting and training the secretaries for the company. He also encouraged me to be innovative. On a trip to the USA I discovered the advertising concept of "Gal Fridays", and started advertising for us in this way. It worked very well. Subsequently I was much involved in headhunting for our clients.'

Learning New Skills

'I began to make quite a contribution to various aspects of work at Binder Hamlyn Fry, especially in the preparation of a digest of the activities of the firm, and editing management reports. I also edited a book on management accounting, when Bob Fry fell ill.

'I learned a great deal; I was sent with a team to help sort out a hotel chain and make it more profitable. I was introduced to various "fiddles" that can go on in the bar. I also began to sell consultancy projects and acquired my own clients.'

Considering Career Turnaround

'Whilst I was working with Binder Hamlyn Fry I met Toby Hyde, an American executive who became my second husband. He was then in the process of buying two advertising agencies and merging them together. After we married, I decided to stop work and have children. We had a son, but by the time he had gone off to prep school and with my husband as Chairman of a public company and away a lot, I missed my business life. Around this time I accompanied my husband on a business trip to Canada and met a friend who ran a successful and very interesting outplacement business. Outplacement was almost unknown then in Britain; I saw at first-hand what it was like for people to be suddenly unemployed, and how useful it was to have a base from which to search for a job and advice for the process of doing so, especially for the many who'd never had to do this before.

'I decided that I wanted to set up my own outplacement business in Britain. I knew I had the potential to do this, because I was given a series of personality tests, and I'm a great believer in how useful these can be. In particular, I had taken the Cattels 16 Personality Factors test, in which I came up strongly as an executive. This gave me the confidence even though I'd never run anything before.'

Taking the Plunge

'It took me about a year to set up my own business, from first thinking about it to opening up shop. At first I tried to copy the business that my friend was running in Canada, which was called "Forty Plus" and specialized in finding jobs for executives over 40 years old who were unemployed or who had been made redundant.

'I approached various big corporations — which I knew might need outplacement services in the future — and asked them for their backing. Amazingly I had a very good response, and gained a lot of support relatively quickly. In the first instance, Bob Haslam (now Lord Haslam) of ICI provided me with free office space, and then Shell and Cadbury-Schweppes donated money and office equipment. I opened my offices in Templar House, High Holborn. My sponsors were intrigued that here was a youngish woman who wanted to help middle-aged executives to get jobs after they'd been sacked.

My husband, meanwhile, retired as Chairman of a public company and I persuaded him to join me.'

Achieving Career Turnaround

'In running my business, and even when it grew and developed so much, I still never borrowed from banks. I expanded only when I could afford to. I don't believe in the concept of using "OPM" — Other People's Money. I had to be a bit of a hustler to gain new business from the corporations, having to convince them that I could solve their problems. Many had never used outplacement before, and I had to persuade them that they really needed my services.

'I was the first woman to run an outplacement company, at a time when there were few such companies in Britain. People soon realized I was not a dilettante, but that I was very serious and determined about running this business and making a success of it. It wasn't always that easy, as there was still a lot of male chauvinism around, although there's less all the time. I received a lot of publicity when I set up my business. *The Observer* did a big, impressive-looking piece entitled 'Pauline Hyde: Interested in Older Men'. I was a bit embarrassed about this at first, but it was all good publicity really.'

Practical Advice

'Speaking for myself and for the many people whom we help to achieve career turnaround, I would say that the qualities needed for career transformation include being a good listener. Like preparing a marketing plan for a new product, you have to market yourself Many people have never really had to do this before.

'We are constantly helping people to achieve career turnaround: probably the majority of people whom we help end up doing something quite different from their previous role, and they are usually happier as a result. We help by giving them an objective assessment of themselves; we help them decide what they want to do and how to go about achieving this. We sometimes get people coming to us who are really traumatized, but in most cases we are able to help people get a better job than the one they left or had to give up.

'We have very many people who have achieved career turnaround in our programmes, and I personally know many others. I believe almost anyone can achieve career turnaround if they really work at it and are given help and encouragement over the time it takes.'

Peter Middleton: Diplomat/Chief Executive, Thomas Cook

'I spent several years in the diplomatic service, in a wide range of Foreign Office appointments, travelling fairly constantly. My last posting was in Paris, and I could have taken on increasingly senior appointments. But I was beginning to find it tiresome to have to move my home base every couple of years, and in any case I had often wondered why I had gone in for the diplomatic service, because I didn't have very much in common with many of my colleagues. So I accepted an opportunity to go into international banking, and this led to my present challenging position heading up Thomas Cook, now part of the Midland Bank Group. It's quite different and in many ways more stimulating, and it does represent an incredible change in activity.'

Background

'I'd no family background in the Foreign Service; I'm closer to a blue-collar or steelworker community. My careers officer at university in Hull, when I told him I had studied in Paris, suggested I go down to the Civil Service selection board. I thought there was very little way that I would have got through. But I did, and then I turned them down when they offered me a job. They sent a guy from their personnel department and he said, "We are very interested to know why you've turned us down," and I said "Well, I just don't think I'd fit in," and he said, "I think you're making a mistake, we really are trying to widen our field of new entrants." So I joined.

'Before I came to Thomas Cook, before I entered the banking world, I wasn't consciously seeking to leave the Foreign Office, but there were some things building up in my mind that were beginning to bother me. I was not particularly impressed by the quality of management in the upper echelons of the Foreign Office. Also, it seemed that the closer I got to the top of my profession, to what I had always perceived of as the really interesting jobs, the more they turned out not to be that interesting at all.

'I then thought to myself, there is a family dimension to this. In order to be fair to children, you really do have to give them stable education from the ages of 13 to 18, and in the diplomatic service that almost always means sending them to boarding school in the UK. The eldest of our three children was by then 14, and we didn't really want to see them only in holiday times. So that was another factor which led me to decide that when I came back from Paris I was going to request that I should not be sent abroad for five years.'

Considering Career Turnaround

'Then the opportunity at Midland came on the horizon, and I decided that if I was going to change this certainly was the moment to do it, and if I was going somewhere other than Whitehall, the City was where I wanted to be.

'I didn't think I had any skills that I could use in the City. I was absolutely amazed that they might be interested in me. Now Hervé de Carmoy, who was then head of Midland International, said that he wanted to experiment to see whether somebody with what he thought of as the traditional values and mental disciplining of Whitehall could be taught banking skills.

'In the French culture there is much more interaction between public servants and business. They get better civil servants as a result and I suspect, maybe, better businessmen. This was what de Carmoy called the Burgundian initiative, because he's from Burgundy. So I was his Burgundian initiative.

'What he then did was to send me off on a tour of Midland International, which was mostly in London, department by department, with two aims in mind: to learn what the departments did and to give him my views on how I felt the thing was organized, run, the spirit in it, etc.

'It took me about a quarter of an hour to make the decision to move to the City, once I got to the point where I was offered the choice.'

Influences and Mentors

'I never really had a mentor, but there were people I admired, such as Peter Carrington, an outstanding, brilliant man to work for. I picked off a lot of things from a lot of people. What I picked off from Peter Carrington was the wonderful inspiration and motivation that people in a senior position can make by just being normal with supposed inferiors. Before Peter Carrington's car was going to leave Paris one morning — we'd been working most of the night and my secretary and one other had been typing for quite a lot of the night — he came into the office and he just sat on the desk, having insisted on coming to thank them. They would have walked across the Channel for him. And that episode has been of great use for me in places like Thomas Cook, making sure I don't cut myself off. I was also influenced by de Carmoy, when the bank job arose, and he helped prepare me to take over banking operations. Since then I have developed enormous respect for Gene Lockhart of Midland and have learned a lot from him.'

Learning New Skills

'Midland had a financial analysis seminar which lasted about three months, and that gave you accountancy skills and financial analysis skills, taught you about cash flow and the rest of it. That was painful, because I was surrounded by very bright 24-year-olds. It equalled itself out though, because the final part of the course is when you take a company to bits and decide what to do with it. They give you an artificial thing like would you lend them £1 million and what would you advise, etc. And that's where wider experience comes in. But that was pretty painful. I was a real slob. But it was great.

Then I went and ran bank operations. It was in a mess, it had too many hierarchical layers, too many senior managers. So I cleared them out, got it sorted out, and I was just starting to build things. We'd just begun my variation on quality circles and stuff like that, and people had got over the trauma of the changes that I'd made, when I was asked to take over the Thomas Cook group and sort that out.

'When you ask if I've had any problem convincing others that I could achieve this change in career, my response is I didn't even stop to think about it. I only do things that I know I'm going to be able to do (I gave up the piano after five lessons a few years ago). I think that's what people see eventually, that you're absolutely determined that you're going to be successful and so are they — and you don't waver.'

The Challenge of Career and Corporate Turnaround

'You have to give people a clear vision of where you're taking the group, and then ask them if they want to come along. If they do then great, and you let them get on with it. It's no more difficult than that. You can't turn a company round sitting behind a desk issuing circulars: you've got to get out and talk to people and you've got to listen to them, you've got to debate things with them so that they understand what you're doing and they've had a chance both to influence it and to test that you really believe in what you're doing, and that it's right. Now with a worldwide company, in about 130 countries, that precludes being at home with your slippers on at 5 p.m., so no, I've never actually seen *Neighbours*. This is 18 hours a day, 7 days a week. That's the way I run it — I'm available, that's the only way I can do it.

'This year for the third year running — for each of the three years that I have been here — we will earn record profits. And at the end of this year, despite a pretty difficult climate in the UK, Germany, Austria, and Canada, our profits will be three times the level that I inherited. In the middle of 1988 when the door was revolving and spinning and we were very close to disaster I made a couple of absolutely magnum mistakes in appointments, and in one region the company was on a knife edge. I wasn't going to stop doing what I knew I had to do, but the consequences were quite dramatic. And there were people digging away under the foundations so that I would fall in. You just have to outlast it, you say "I'm sorry, I'm not stopping."

'I've tried to create a company more determined to be successful than any other company in our industry and maybe many others. I mean this year in the UK the market's 30 per cent down and our revenues are 20 per cent up, because we're not giving in — just not giving in. We made more profit last year than our five nearest rivals put together in the UK. If I knew how I'd done it I'd write a book.

'On 5 July 1991, we're 150 years old, and I want to be able to say "trust us worldwide" and know that the customers can. There is a buzz in the company now, it's great, even in large centres like the UK headquarters in Peterborough, which has some 1500 people.'

Practical Advice

'When I hire people, I take their technical skills as read, but just these are not enough. I look for two qualities in people: one is guts, and the other one is that their chemistry fits with the other people in the team so that there is no one with a private agenda. The problems we underwent in 1988 arose because I deviated from these rules.

'You're reduced to one or two pretty simple things that would help others in a similar position to mine, and I'm not sure there's a way of writing them down which avoids them appearing as clichés. It seems to me that the first requirement is absolute honesty. You really have to be honest with people, because otherwise they're never going to trust you, and a company without trust will not be successful. Technical skills are really secondary to relationship skills in many instances.

'Somebody thinking of a career change has got to make sure they know themselves thoroughly, they've got to know what their strengths and weaknesses are and they've got to assess candidly so far as they are able, whether the range of strengths they have match what is going to be required in their new career.'

Reviewing the Situation

'From where I came from — Middlesbrough — there was a certain mystique about the Foreign Office and the City.

'I can't stand people who are falsely modest. If you're intelligent and you pretend that you're not, then you've got some real problems inside of yourself, haven't you? I know I'm intelligent, so what? I didn't arrange it, I didn't achieve it — it was given so I used it — and I'm proud of that. When you get in to the Foreign Office and you see the people who are in it, there are some excellent people there, some high-quality human beings and some very clever people and sometimes a combination of both. But it's not that special — it's different from Middlesbrough, but it's not that special.'

'The single most difficult thing moving from the Foreign Office to Midland Bank was that I had earned a certain reputation in the Foreign Office which had built up because I'd done reasonably well, but in Midland I had nothing — I was unknown and it's very difficult — it's almost impossible overnight to move from an organization where a lot of people know you and you know where you fit in to an equally pretty large organization where you've got to go in and build a reputation.'

Dr John Polkinghorne, Physicist/ Clergyman

'I've really had two career changes, and have done three different things. My original career was as a theoretical physicist, using mathematics to understand the smallest bits of matter and their behaviour. And in between my present job and leaving physics in 1979 I trained for ordination, was ordained into the Ministry of the Church of England, and spent five years working in the parochial ministry: that was the biggest change. And now I've come back into the academic world in a rather unexpected way, and I continue to write about science and theology.'

Background

'I thought for a long time that I probably wouldn't remain simply a theoretical physicist all my life. The reason for that is that in these mathematically-based subjects you lose originality as you grow older. Your mind becomes less flexible, and after about 27 years in the subject I began to feel I'd done what I could for it. Obviously I could continue to do the same old tricks, but I thought it rather unlikely that I would do something that was new in any significant way. I'd foreseen that this would happen because it tends to happen — not with everybody, but it's a very common experience.

'So for a long time I'd planned that when that began to happen — when the subject began to move away from me — I wouldn't stay in it just hanging on. And as I approached my 50th birthday, I began to feel the time had come to do something about that.'

Considering Career Turnaround

'It didn't follow from that that I became a clergyman, but I've always been part of the believing, worshipping community, so it was something to think about. I'd been a lay reader for a few years, so I'd had the experience of doing a little bit of preaching and helping with conducting worship, and I'd enjoyed that. I've always enjoyed working with people. And I began to think about what I might do. I began to talk to my wife about it — it was very much a joint decision, obviously. The idea of seeking ordination began to develop quite quickly over a period of a few months, without any terrific drama or tremendous crisis or anything like that. Fortunately we saw eye to eye about it.

'So I then had to have my vocation tested: the church has a selection procedure for which you have to sign up. And that was helpful and reassuring, that other people who didn't know me but who were experienced and perceptive would decide whether this was a sensible decision for me, and whether I had a calling to do it and wasn't just experiencing some sort of middle-aged crisis. And so I went through that, and I was impressed actually with the thoroughness and the care with which the Church looked at me. The people connected with the selection procedure were not just dazzled by the thought of a Fellow of the Royal Society becoming a clergyman. But they said yes; so I trained, and went off into the parochial ministry.'

Influences and Mentors

'Obviously I talked to one or two of my close friends about my decision, and I do have a close friend who is both a clergyman and a psychotherapist. He understands about human motivation from his work, and I did particularly seek his advice, and found him helpful, but by and large I think the decision was principally my own and my wife's.

'Actually, at the same time my wife was engaged in her own middle-aged career adventure. She'd done a maths degree at Cambridge (that's where we met) and worked as a statistician for a little while before we got married. So while I was training to become a clergyman, she trained to become a nurse. This was good in many ways because we propped each other up when necessary.'

Reactions from Colleagues

'At the time I was running a fairly large research group and had five or six senior colleagues working with me. I remember very vividly the day when I told my colleagues I was going to resign my professorship. It was quite a dramatic moment: it came at the end of a meeting about something else, and came out of the blue as far as they were concerned. They were stunned first of all, but after that they were on the whole supportive. One or two people obviously thought I was doing something pretty weird. My closest senior colleague said to me that he wouldn't have guessed I was going to do it, but if I had ever mentioned I was thinking of leaving the academic world he would have guessed I would become a clergyman. That was quite nice in a way.

'During this period, I travelled around visiting laboratories, and people would say to me quite often, "John, why are you doing it?" And we would have interesting, sometimes quizzical conversations about that. It was clearly a slightly eccentric thing to do.'

Learning New Skills

'It was very funny becoming a student again, and the strangest part of training for my new career was my two years in theological college, because I'd been university teaching for 25 years or more, and to sit listening to a lecture rather than giving it was much more difficult than I had expected.

'Naturally, I kept thinking to myself "will I be good at being a clergyman?" I like trying to explain things to people, I'm quite interested in people and quite a sympathetic listener. I carried these traits over from the teaching side of my career in the university to the preaching and pastoral aspects of my career as a clergyman, so there was a continuity there.

'I had to acquire quite a lot of knowledge for my new career. Obviously I had to study theology, which I'd read in a desultory way before, but hadn't studied very systematically, and I spent two years in theological college doing that. There are lots of things about being a clergyman that you can only learn by doing it, and it's part of the system that you serve an apprenticeship, which is called your *title*.'

Sacrifices

'I did make financial sacrifices in so far that I gave up my professor's job and professor's salary, so clearly our financial circumstances changed quite sharply. When I became a student my college, which in those days was Trinity College, very kindly allowed me to go back to being a teaching fellow — not in the university but in the college — so in fact I worked my way through Westcott House. The whole time I was a student I would go up the road and turn into a Don and do teaching for Trinity. I earned a reasonable amount, not as much as I had earned a professor of course, but enough to pay my course fees and to keep us in a satisfactory state at home.

'We moved into a smaller house, partly for economic reasons and partly to be nearer Westcott House. And we already had a lot of this world's goods; we had books and pictures and furniture, all that sort of thing.

'My wife was a student as well — a student nurse — and was being paid as such, not a great amount. Still, as I said, finance was not a problem for us, though I can see that for a young curate starting a family it would be.'

Changes and Contrasts

'When I became a clergyman the biggest change for me was that most of the work I did was from home. I spent a lot of time visiting people, but home was my base, I could see people at home and I would obviously do my work and write my sermons at home. That was unusual for me, I'd always had the experience of going out to work, and in fact I preferred it. I quite like the separation between work and home.

'Being a clergyman I had much more contact with people, and obviously it was a much wider range of people — you never knew who you were going to be in contact with. You can find yourself dealing with all sorts of different people, old or young, some desperate, some complacent, all sorts. They may well be intelligent people, but by and large in a parish they're not particularly academic people, and I did miss that. I missed the stimulus of intellectual conversation. I missed the cultural side of college life, the setting in which you share many common things that you know about, common names that you can use in conversation and people understand who they are.

'One of the big differences between the academic world and the parish world is that the academic world has this rhythm of term and vacation. Term time is very busy, particularly here at Cambridge because we have such short terms, but then you have a long vacation when things slow down, and you have a lot of time to devote to your own work, writing books. Parish life has a different rhythm altogether, it just keeps chugging along, you can never turn it off, it's always there. So I did quite miss the rhythm of term and vacation, and I was quite pleased to get back to it. This rhythm provides a flexibility that parish life doesn't, it's totally different.

'When I entered the parish life I also had far less time to read and think about things, which had always been a very large part of my life. I've always thought it important that clergy do make some space to take something in; they shouldn't always be dishing out. After I was a curate I was then licensed to "go solo," and I became a vicar of a very nice smallish village of about 2,500 people, down in Kent, I enjoyed that very much and I even had a bit of spare time there, as opposed to when I'd been a curate in a large working class parish in South Bristol — I really was very busy then.'

'It had been strange going from Cambridge to Bristol. It wasn't a rough area, but it wasn't a prosperous area either, for it was entirely working class, an area where people lived in the house that mum and dad had bought for £300 in 1930. It was a very stable area and very neighbourly in consequence. I'd never lived in a big town before yet where our parish was felt just like a village, it had that sort of neighbourly feel of a village. I hadn't realized before that you could have that in a big town.

'Wearing a clerical collar was the main change in my appearance. I was encouraged to wear it all the time, and I did actually in my parish, except on my day off. You can argue it both ways. Some people say it's very awkward — for example if you get on a train, the quickest way of having a compartment to yourself is to wear a clerical collar, because people don't want to come in! But round about the parish or in the village, I found a clerical collar actually very helpful. First of all, it told people who I was and it gave me a kind of instant access to them. I could knock on any door. You could just talk to people. If I walked round the village, I would say hello to people everywhere, and if they looked as though they might want to exchange a few words I'd stop. It was very interesting in Bristol, because it was a biggish parish there. On my day off I'd sometimes forget that I wasn't wearing a clerical collar and smile at people and they would be much more wary because they didn't know who I was. With a clerical collar they still might not really know who I was, but they would recognize my "insignia", as it were.'

A Second Turnaround

'While I was in Kent, after I'd been in the parish for about two years as a vicar, I wrote a book, one of the first of my books on science and religion. I could see that in the longer term, parish life was not going to allow me do as much writing as I wanted to do. I had developed the feeling, which I hadn't been aware of at the beginning, that part of my ministry would be to write in the area of science and religion, and contribute in this way.

'So I went to see my bishop — the Bishop of Dover — and explained all this to him. I said I was very happy in my parish but that I felt that in the longer term I would like a job that had a more academic component to it, with less of a pastoral side. He agreed, and I thought I would be making a change in about two or three years time.

'Within a few months of that conversation, quite out of the blue, I was rung up and eventually offered the job of being the Dean of Trinity Hall. That meant being the parish priest of a college, but with an academic component to it as well. I didn't know what to do because I'd only been in the parish for just over two years, which is too short a time really to consider leaving. I went to see the bishop to talk to him about it and he said "you've been offered the job that you've described to me, and I think you ought to think carefully about accepting it." So I thought about it, and I did take it in the end, and that put me back in the academic world again.'

Considering Career Turnaround

'So I was back in the academic world, but in an entirely new role. I'd been a professor and I came back as a dean, which is a different job altogether. I was in Trinity Hall for three years, and I enjoyed it very much. Then just as my third year was coming to an end I was rung up, again out of the blue, and asked whether I would like to be considered for the vacancy of President of Queens' College, which very much surprised me. I said I'd be prepared to be considered, but I would need to think about it very carefully.

'Eventually, after a series of interviews, it became fairly clear to me that it was quite possible that I'd be offered the job. I had to think very seriously about this, because being head of a House is a secular job. Most heads of Houses are just lay people — not priests — and I had to decide whether it was the right job for a priest to take. I didn't get ordained with the idea of becoming a head of House.'

A Combination of Careers

'This third role has been possible for me partly because every college has a chapel, so we have a dean and a chaplain here, and they are kind enough to let me play a part in chapel worship. So I haven't lost that dimension to my life, although obviously it has been diminished.

I continue to write about religion, so I continue that sort of ministry. In the vacation time I talk in church groups about the problems in belief. I find it very odd: here I am back in the academic world with an entirely different role in a place I never expected I'd end up.

'I now combine my interests by writing about science and religion. They are different, but there are certain continuities. What I need to do is try and understand how the world view of science and the world view of theology relate to each other. It's one single world they're trying to describe. The thing that concerns me the most, and has concerned me throughout my whole career, is to search for the truth, both in science and religion. This is the most important question, and we have to consider different views.

'Both science and religion involve acts of judgment of some sort. Of course, there are differences: in science you can do experiments and repeat them, whilst personal encounters — whether it's between people or between a person and God — are unrepeatable, they happen, and their meaning then has to be found on that unique occasion. That makes for quite considerable differences, but I'm absolutely opposed to the view that science is reasonable and religion blind assertion: shutting the eyes and gritting the teeth, while you assert the impossible. So in that sense I don't see great discontinuities between my career as a scientist and my present career as some sort of theologian.'

Practical Advice

'You've got to want to do it first of all, that's the most important thing. Motivation is the key, and there was both a push and a pull for me. I don't know whether it's humility or realism or whatever it is, but you have to accept that you are likely to make a transition from perhaps being reasonably significant and responsible in one career to starting at the bottom of something else.

'I also feel it is important to have help from people other than your friends. Obviously you want to discuss any career change with your family and friends, but it is also quite helpful to have somebody who doesn't know you beforehand, who is not going to think "I'll just go along with John and support whatever he wants to do."

'I think Britain has a very inflexible society. We're inflexible in two ways: it's thought undesirable to move on to do something else, and even within a particular profession there is a ratchet mechanism that decrees that you can only move upwards. In actual fact, for many people it would sensible to move upwards for a while and then downwards again. Even in the academic world I think that would be quite sensible. There are certain times in life when you welcome responsibility, and certain times when you might want to give it up. There are times when you need quite a lot of money, when your family's growing up, and other times when you don't need so much. So even within a profession it would be sensible not always to move higher and higher.'

Reviewing the Situation

'I think I've now come to rest after all my changes. First of all, we've moved around far too much in the last ten years. I've been a student, a curate, a vicar, and a dean of a college chapel, and each of those involved moves. My wife and I both now want a settled life. Secondly, this is a job that one doesn't do just for a year or two; it's a very serious job. And by the time I've done a few years at this job I shall be at retirement age, so I think this is my resting place.

'Like anyone who makes a change in middle life, you're a curious combination of things. Academically I'm quite a senior person, but among the clergy I'm not particularly. I have experience, but not an enormous amount, so I doubt whether I'd ever have been offered a senior position back in the clergy.

'I still officiate at weddings, christenings and funerals, as I have an opportunity to do that, and I lend a hand with doing the services in the college chapel. We have a few weddings in the college, and I'm pleased to help with that when needed. Occasionally I am asked to baptize the children of friends of mine, which I like doing, and indeed I baptized my own two grandchildren — I enjoyed that most of all.

'I suppose I've discovered more clearly that you can help people simply by listening to them. Indeed, it's often the only thing you can do. I've learnt more how to be still and quiet, and sometimes I try to help other people to do those things as well, and that's been important to me.

'Anyone making a transition occasionally feels nostalgic for the old way of life, and will ask themselves whether they've done the right thing. It would be very odd really to proceed without any doubt at all. Yet I must say I never let myself feel paralysed by those doubts; I thought I was doing the right thing, and looking back on it I feel very much that I did, and I'm glad I did it. It was a worthwhile thing for me to have done.'

Dr Erling Refsum: Orthopaedic Surgeon/ Stockbroker

'I qualified as a doctor and then as a surgeon, but for the last few years I've been working as a stockbroker, more specifically, as a pharmaceuticals analyst for a large Japanese securities house. The two careers are certainly a great deal different. Of course, I did use pharmaceuticals as a doctor, but I didn't then know very much about the pharmaceutical companies themselves. I enjoy my work in the City, but making the transition was quite a challenge, and I still on occasion miss my old life in surgery.'

Background

'Everyone in my family seems to be either a doctor or a teacher, so from the usual background of school I went straight into Guy's Medical School, almost automatically, to train as a doctor. I qualified, then trained as a surgeon and was very happy working in orthopaedics. As far as my career turnaround was concerned, it wasn't any one particular thing that changed everything overnight, but more a collection of circumstances and one particularly interesting offer made to me.

'I loved the work in orthopaedic surgery and it was deeply satisfying, but the hours were gruelling. My home life was limited, and the pay and prospects in the NHS were also limited. Then I got very lucky, in that a friend made me an offer I virtually couldn't refuse. He had already blazed the trail by leaving medicine himself and moving very successfully into the City. Would I join him? Surgery gives you a certain confidence in your own abilities, and the move wasn't totally irreversible, so I decided to give it a try.

'It wasn't a lightning decision or any kind of conversion on the road to Damascus. It was more a gradual build-up of frustration and bone-weary tiredness, combined with the interest of doing something new. For the previous nine years I had only averaged two free days a fortnight, and had hardly any sleep on the other nights. The stress was affecting my health. Put it this way: I only managed to quit smoking when I stopped working as a surgeon.'

Considering Career Turnaround

'The whole career turnaround process really began for me in about 1986, with a transitional phase lasting about one year during which I almost slipped into business accidentally. I didn't deliberately plan events, but at the time I was trying to develop some surgical instruments that I had invented. My son had developed febrile convulsions at that time, and I had an idea for a gadget that would prevent this condition.

'I then went on a course offered by the London Business School on starting up a small business; my intention was to develop this gadget. I found the course fascinating, and it gave me my first inkling of what business was about. Unfortunately by then I had run out of money, and had to devote myself to surgery again. Thankfully my son's fits had stopped, and in any case someone else developed my gadget. However, as my first real introduction to business the course had been fun and had opened my eyes a bit more to the world outside medicine.

'About that time I had already thought quite a bit about setting up a business, so that when my friend asked me to join him in stockbroking, I was already well-disposed towards the idea. So I tried it, liked it, and have stayed with it ever since.

'The nearest thing to planning that I ever did was on the LBS course when we were taught about applying goal-setting, time-management and prioritization schedules to our own lives. I had never used any of these techniques formally before, although I realized that I was already applying their principles automatically in day-to-day surgery. The time-planning techniques turned out to be particularly useful. The simple act of actually writing down a list of words or a jumbled page full of ideas about what you want and then sorting them into some order of importance clears your thoughts wonderfully, so that you feel better straight away.'

The Benefit of Experience

'At this point I didn't think about my strengths and weaknesses, the skills I had and didn't have. I mean, surgery was all I really knew about, and although it gives you a great deal of confidence about facing anything put in front of you, one could ask whether operating on people is really a good training for doing anything else.

'On the positive side, I never worried much about my abilities. Looking back, surgery does give one great leadership training as well as the chance to gain experience in problem-solving and decision-making. Surgeons are generally used to making decisions by themselves and quickly, then carrying them through and dealing with the consequences. The job demands it. You are forced to stick by your decisions whether they turn out to be right or wrong, so you naturally tend to become a fairly forceful character.

'However, on the negative side, surgery certainly didn't help me develop any tact. Since entering the business world I have had to consciously tone down my habitual approach. I have had to learn to use gentler, more persuasive manners. For example, if I was operating and asked for a scalpel but got forceps, the offending instrument usually rapidly ended up somewhere on the other side of the operating theatre and the volume of my voice and level of impatience would increase. You can't behave like that in business, which was a difficult lesson to learn.

'Of my old skills the most useful was probably my ability to gather information, which the study of medicine encourages. Interviewing patients, asking them lots of questions and trying to find out what's wrong with them teaches you to collect and collate a mass of relevant information. The main difference is that the patients were usually willing to tell me anything I asked for, whereas in the City people and companies are more reticent. Thinking on my feet and building up mental pictures about problems is much the same in medicine as it is in business.'

Learning New Skills

'Inside the first two days of beginning work as a stockbroker I was sent away on a course to teach me the basics of accounting and finance, so that I could sit the necessary stock exchange exams. I hadn't done this sort of studying for years, and I didn't know about some of the most elementary ideas, which was very embarrassing. Medicine is quiet a hermetically sealed world, where money plays little part in your main occupation, which is supposed to be caring for your patients. So initially I was comparatively ignorant about the world I'd stepped into.

'While on this course I had a deluge of information thrown at me. In fact, this sort of information overload was exactly what I was used to from my years with the NHS, and consequently it was precisely this aspect of my new career I felt happiest with, initially. The rest of it was more difficult. The main shock was my realization of how little I knew about what other people seemed to take for granted. I felt as if I was always asking very simple and dumb questions, such as "What are we trying to do?" "Why and how do we do it?" and "What tools do we have to do it with?" The people I was training with must have got really fed up with these very basic questions.

'Because I had only a slight understanding of the whole thing I had to start at the very beginning. For instance, in the beginning I often asked myself "What is the point of a company?" I learned that basically the point is to make money. It took me about three months just to fully understand that. From these beginnings I developed the habit of constantly questioning, actively seeking out new knowledge about the business and trying always to learn more about it.

'I found that people were very tolerant of the fact that I was learning. I was working for a company which is well-known for taking a very long-term view, and the friend who had invited me in had undergone the same transition, so he understood my problems. Both the company and my boss knew there was going to have to be a training period, and they made allowances for this. I was given the time and the opportunity to learn things, which was most important to me. If I had gone into business by myself I might have had to learn faster. The pressure would have been greater, and I would probably have made more mistakes. Initially I did make some mistakes, as do all novices. But frankly, if you're not making occasional mistakes, then you're not learning anything, and you're not trying hard enough.'

Changes and Contrasts

'Initially the financial differences were marginal, but City salaries tend to rise faster and higher than in medicine, although the risks of losing your job are also dramatically increased. The best thing for me has been the company car, which meant that for the first time in my life I had a new car. In medicine you never really notice any lack of money because you're working all the time and don't have time to spend it!

'To a certain extent moving to a completely new role has a rejuvenating effect. I'd been a surgeon for nine years, and frankly I was finding that one operation was much the same as another: exciting but repetitive. Having to change to something completely different is like having a holiday, and for the first few months I was quite euphoric about the whole thing, but then I had to start learning new skills and fitting in with everyone else.

'It took a while before I felt up to scratch in the City. I've been here for four years now, and I still do not feel as much in charge as I did in medicine. However, the mentality which drove me in surgery does not allow me to sit back and be average; I'm always thinking "That's not good enough, I have to get better".

'Life certainly changed after my career turnaround. I now wear a suit every day, instead of bloodstained operating clothes and a white coat. I spend more time socializing, and my alcohol intake has increased dramatically. I work different hours. When I arrived at the City, the hours were no longer nine to five, they were more like eight to eight — but this was still a good five hours shorter than my normal working day in medicine. I get to sleep every night, I get to sleep all through the night, and every weekend I can do what I please. My free time has more than doubled. Mainly because of this business does not rule my life as much as surgery did.

'I work with a different group of people now. I've exchanged the hospital mess with its collective support for a much more individual and politically aware free-for-all. If I think of the advantages and disadvantages of my new career compared with my old one, I find I've got double the amount of freedom and double the salary now, but only half the respect and half the security. However, rather than being narrowly focussed on medicine my horizons are now much wider, and my overall career prospects are much better. The potential to achieve is much greater now, although one must remember the constant lack of security. Many of the friends I've made in the City have found themselves on the streets with hardly a day's notice.'

Reactions from Colleagues

'The most interesting thing about people's reactions was the difference between those of the City people and those working in medicine. Doctor friends said "Well done, you've managed to get out!", while City people said "How on earth could you have left medicine?" The hardest person of all to convince was my mother. It took her about three years to come to terms with it all, although both my wife and parents were always very supportive. Actually, I think it was only when she saw me on TV talking about a pharmaceutical company that she finally accepted that my change of career had been a good idea.'

Practical Advice

'On reflection, I think the quality that helped me most during the first year was my own sheer pig-headedness and drive to keep going. There were times during the first year when I was thoroughly miserable. If you're a surgeon you have authority and a pride in what you're doing. To jump from that to being cack-handed and stupid at the bottom of the pile is quite demeaning. I found it very annoying: I just hated being ignorant, it made me angry and quite depressed for a while. Then I realized that the only answer was to keep learning, and eventually it all improved.

'Being a newcomer to the business is a bit like being a convert. You are always a bit more zealous than the old hands. By constant studying you actually start to overtake those who've been at it for years and haven't looked at the basics for a long time nor paid enough attention to the new ideas coming into the industry. Becoming good at my new job was a long grind, but I was used to hard work.

'If I was asked to offer advice to others who are contemplating career turnaround, I'd say you need enough self-confidence and sheer bloody-mindedness to keep going when things get miserable. Do not give up, keep battling away, because the harder it is, and the more effort you put into it, the more worthwhile the feeling is when you get through it. No pain, no gain. Just remember, if it's hard for you, it's probably equally hard for everybody else, so that if you're working away at it and they're not, you'll eventually end up better than them.'

Gerry Roche: Marketing Director/ Executive Recruiter

'Having started out as a management trainee with AT & T, I then took a similar role with ABC Television, moving through all the departments there. Later I joined Kordite and became Director of Marketing. After a few years with that organization I was recruited to Heidrick and Struggles, which was, even at that time, one of the top four executive search firms in the United States. So my career has spanned telecommunications, broadcasting, plastics and executive search.'

Background

'When Heidrick and Struggles came after me, I had been head of marketing for the largest polyethylene manufacturing company in the US. Initially the recruiter approached me to go with Mill Print, another plastics manufacturer and a division of Philip Morris. The assignment was to recruit a Vice-President, in charge of marketing, to be based in Minneapolis. At that precise moment in history, John F. Kennedy was killed.

'I don't mean to get melodramatic but I was very much a Kennedy enthusiast and his death disillusioned me a great deal. At the same time, Kordite was purchased by Mobil. Here was this big New York oil company acquiring this snappy, entrepreneurial plastics company. I wasn't sure about the idea of being in a big corporation, and I also didn't like the folks from Mill Print telling me "You're going to be part of Philip Morris."'

'I was put off by the big company approach. I began to ask myself, "What's life all about, what do I want to do, and what do I want to be?" And that's when the recruiter said to me, "Why won't you take this job at Philip Morris?" I said, "I don't know, I just don't . . ." — "Why do you want to leave Kordite?" the recruiter asked. Again I said, "I don't know . . ."

'He then said to me "You sound confused." I admitted that I was. That was when he suggested that I come in and work for Heidrick and Struggles while I was looking for something else. After thinking it over, I decided that I would. I've been here for 26 years and I'm still looking!'

Reactions from Colleagues

'When I chose to go with Heidrick and Struggles from what was now a division of Mobil my friends and family thought I was crazy. They didn't understand my reasoning. They didn't understand the business. I'd graduated from college with honours, completed a master's degree with honours, and went on to become an officer in the Navy . . .I was hot stuff. They were expecting me to be the greatest thing that ever came down the pipe. "And you're going to do *what?*" they asked, "You're going into personnel agency work?" People didn't know what it was then. Today my attitude is that the people who count know what's going on and know who we are. I don't deal with anybody who isn't the best, and that's all there is to it. We get paid to find exceptional people and, as a result, I deal with exceptional people day-in and day-out. For example, the guy who was sitting in that chair before you came in is the chairman of a billion-dollar company. He's dynamite. We're working on an exciting, growth-orientated situation right now that may be perfect for him . . .and that's exciting to me.

'It's hard to tell you how I convinced other people that I could be a recruiter, and make a success of it. If you ask me when people stopped criticizing me, or stopped being shocked about what I was doing, or if I ever began to think it was not quite a good idea, I'd have to say I honestly don't know. I'm not trying to be coy or cute, but I never cared. I did what I wanted to do and I made a living out of it. I also worked with a lot of good people, expanded the New York office and made the firm grow. I never sat around worrying about what people thought of me. But I'll tell you whom I do care about — my clients. I care about what they think of me. That's what drives me. My guiding principle is perfection for clients.'

The Challenges of a New Career

'I never skimp on a job, and I won't let anybody I work with skimp on a job. I get negative feedback when I've placed someone who doesn't work out. Years ago, I placed the CEO at RCA; ultimately, he committed suicide. I get paid for my judgment of people, and when my judgment is wrong I can't say "Well, the wind blew the wrong way," or "It's tough luck," or "The economy went sour." When a guy doesn't work out it means I didn't do my job correctly.

'More recently, we worked on a pretty tough search involving a major footwear company. I received a call from the owner: he wanted me to find his replacement. He said he wanted to get out of the business and turn the reins over to someone else, someone strong enough to succeed him. We found the person; he was then hired. Two years later, our placement says to the owner "OK, you promised me I could run this thing, now move over." The bottom line is that our guy has since left and the owner still runs the company. How do you think I feel talking to that person today? You can't tell me that I didn't do something wrong there. I should have known that the owner didn't intend to step down, that he had a hidden agenda.

'It's not unlike when a patient dies on the operating table. Imagine the surgeon coming out of the operating room and saying, "I ran into some unexpected things in there. Hey guys, I'm only human." There's too much rationalization in the search industry. Too many recruiters go around making excuses, saying, "Well, I didn't fill the position, but they hired somebody from within so that's OK", or "The placement didn't work out but it was that client's fault, he was irascible" or "Conditions just changed." Good or bad, we bear responsibility. If we go uptown with the clients, we had better be ready to go downtown with them, too.'

Changes and Contrasts

'When asked about the advantages and disadvantages of search work compared with my previous career, I am reminded of a talk I once gave. I called it "The Agony and Ecstasy of Executive Recruiting." You know what the ecstasy is; the agony of it is that if you're any good you're constantly on call. I bleed when somebody doesn't do the right thing, or if the wrong person gets the job, but I can't force my clients on whom to hire.

'During the first few years in recruiting, I looked hard at all the assignments. Yet I began to like this business, and began to think I could build it up. There are a lot of things going for search work: I like the freedom; I like working with the human element, I like being around people who are capable, special, exceptional . . .and I like making a difference.

'Compared with what I had been doing, recruiting is much more rewarding. I didn't find a whole lot of satisfaction developing polyethylene film and then selling it to the food companies as wrapping for lettuce. That wasn't necessarily the most influential thing I could be doing.'

Reviewing the Situation

'My motivation — the thing that makes me effective — is that I'm anxious. I worry. I care about the client and his or her needs. In this job you can't sit back. You must be constantly on your toes. Even if I say to myself, "Gee I want to relax a little. I'll turn down the valve on generating business and take a break." But, one break and a major assignment can sour. There's just no slowing down.

'The best part of my job is the opportunity to mix with the privileged elite, the high achievers. I never get tired because I love working with these movers and the shakers. That's what turns me on . . .that's the ecstasy.'

John Sculley: Chief Executive, Pepsi Cola/Chief Executive, Apple Computers

'My career turnaround from Pepsi to Apple was provoked when Steve Jobs of Apple asked me: "Do you want to spend the rest of your life selling sugared water, or do you want a chance to change the world?" When he issued this challenge I turned my back on everything I had struggled to achieve at PepsiCo. I was at the top of America's corporate marines; at 38 I was Pepsi's youngest president, and had masterminded the "Pepsi Generation" campaign, which toppled Coke as the number-one brand for the first time in history. Arguably, I helped change the rules of how marketing is practised.

'Suddenly I found myself hypnotized by the fabulous success of Apple, and I was lured by the chance to be a mentor to the man I consider to be the Thomas Edison of our time. I discarded corporate orthodoxy for a very different life. Apple is now a leading player at the sharp end of America's computer business.'

Background

'In the spring of 1978 Pepsi was number one, the leading revenue producer of more than 20,000 items sold in any supermarket. We then had captured 30.8 per cent of the national market to Coke's 29.2

per cent, a slice of business worth more than $3 billion. My fixation on this goal had surfaced as soon as I joined the company as a trainee in 1967. In 1970, I became at the age of 30 Pepsi's youngest marketing vice-president. If I was brash or ignorant on my way to the top, it mattered little to me. I was an impatient perfectionist.

'The cola wars had long pierced the popular culture, touching the lives of everyone from the corner grocer to the inhabitants of the White House. When President Nixon took up residence on Pennsylvania Avenue, Coke vending machines disappeared, but when President Carter arrived the Pepsi machines went out. The politics of the leaders permeated the culture of the companies. Coke was a company whose roots were in the South. Coke executives were true Southern gentlemen. Pepsi was a two-fisted, self-made Republican corporation from the East coast.'

Mentors and Influences

'Don Kendall had become chief executive of Pepsi-Cola in 1963, at which time it was a modestly profitable soft-drink company with $300 million in sales. Some 21 years later, in 1986, Kendall retired as chairman from a highly profitable $9 billion corporation with dominant power in beverages, snacks, and fast foods. He achieved this growth through boldness and risk-taking, forging one of the most successful mergers in American business history in 1965 with Frito-Lay, the Dallas-based snack-food maker; a move which resulted in the founding of PepsiCo.

'Don became a close friend and mentor to me. I had planned to study architecture to become an industrial designer, with the goal of someday opening my own design firm. While I was a graduate student at the University of Pennsylvania's School of Architecture, however, Kendall convinced me my career was not destined to be in architecture but rather in marketing. I would visit him at home and overhear his conversations with ever-present Pepsi colleagues. Then we would sit around till late in the evening discussing them. Kendall said he thought I had good instincts for marketing.

'Kendall's advice prompted a switch to Wharton, the university's graduate school of business. I joined Pepsi-Cola in 1967 as their first MBA.'

Considering Career Turnaround

'After several successes, including launching the "Pepsi Generation" ad campaign with its theme "You've got a lot to live, and Pepsi's got a lot to give" and the "Pepsi Challenge" — the first commercial showed an old Southerner sipping two colas. The masks were ripped off the bottles to reveal that his choice had been Pepsi even though he'd claimed to be a life-long Coke drinker. "Pepsi-Cola!" he exclaims, "Well, I'll be darned!" — I then left to head up Pepsi-Cola's international operations in 1973. What I didn't yet know was how restless I had become.

'As president of Pepsi-Cola, I got a lot of calls from headhunters. But only one headhunter could attract my attention. He was Gerry Roche, a charming, gregarious man, and a headhunter extraordinaire. I had known him as a friend for years. He'd tried to interest me in a number of companies over the years, but I had no interest in any of these jobs. Pepsi was my life. Gerry, however, is no quitter. He called me at Pepsi two days before Thanksgiving Day in 1982 and said, "I know that you're not interested in outside jobs. And you know I wouldn't call unless it was something that was very important. There is something that I think you have got to let me tell you about."

'He told me he was searching for a chief executive for Apple Computer Inc. in California's Silicon Valley. I didn't know very much about the company, although I had purchased one of their computers for my office, and was experimenting with setting up an information network among the bottlers. I was hardly interested in the job however, and told him so.

'Gerry asked me if I would meet the guys at Apple, and sent me a package of information about the company. Inside was a copy of the company's latest annual report and a 10-month-old issue of *Time* magazine. On the cover was a boyish-looking Steve Jobs; the red apple balanced atop his head was being split by an arrow-shaped laser beam. The story, on "America's Risk Takers," positively gushed about how the mustachioed Jobs had practically created the personal computer industry single-handed. It told an amazing tale of a passionate folk-hero whose enduring dream was to allow individuals the power that at present only large corporations and institutions were able to wield. He accomplished this by personalizing the computer — once a distant, nearly ominous abstraction in the form of large main frames, he had brought it down to scale so it could rest on a person's desk top. Six years before Apple's headquarters was located in the bedroom and garage of his parents' home in Los Altos, California. In 1982 it was a *Fortune 500* company.

'Gerry wasted no time filling in the details of his assignment. Apple Computer's board of directors believed that Steve Jobs, Apple's 27-year-old chairman and co-founder, was too inexperienced to be chief executive. "He wants to find someone who is really great, someone he can learn from. The new chief executive reports directly to the board. Steve is focused largely on product development. They're looking for someone who is smart, good at marketing, flexible enough to work in a very different culture, and has international experience. They've been searching for many months and they've looked at a lot of people. But let me tell you, you are the only guy I know who fits all those criteria. I don't have anyone else."

'I had been planning a trip to the West coast to visit my children from my first marriage, so I told Gerry I would visit Apple, but without this meaning I was under any obligation. My kids were very excited at the thought of me meeting Steve Jobs. Now, my kids had grown up in a Hollywood environment; they went to school with the sons and daughters of movie stars. Celebrities couldn't turn their heads. But the mere mention of Steve Jobs seemed something else.

'I was taken aback when I finally met Jobs in the company's two-storey wood-frame building with its shingled roof. It seemed more appropriate for the branch office of an insurance firm than the executive office of a fast-rising corporation. But there were a surprising number of very flash cars in the adjacent parking lot — one sporting a licence plate reading THX APPL.

'Steve was quiet until I began speaking about how I hoped to use the Apple II Plus computer to communicate with Pepsi bottlers. "We are going to make it even better," he enthused "We've got some incredible ideas which will revolutionize the way people use computers. Apple is going to be the most important computer company in the world, far more important than IBM."

'I thought Apple was different from anything I'd seen before. On my flight back to New York I outlined my concepts of what a personal computer should be able to do. I began to realize that when Pepsi created the "Pepsi Generation" we were selling to teenagers, and the campaign had continued to appeal to the same people as they hit their 20s. Now this Pepsi generation was old enough to buy computers for themselves and for their kids at school. I began to think that Apple had the opportunity to create an "Apple Generation".

'Yet I still wasn't interested in leaving Pepsi. After all, I was one of the few people deemed a serious contender to succeed Kendall as Chairman. But every three or four days I would get a call from either Gerry or Steve. Steve would say, "My dream is that every person in the world will have his or her own Apple Computer. To do that we have got to be a great marketing company. You really understand marketing. Since meeting you I'm taken with the idea of an Apple

Generation. I really want us to get to know each other better because I just have a feeling that this could be very important for all of us."

'Steve then came to visit me at Pepsi-Cola, and I explained how important it was for an underdog to convey a leadership image through quality advertising. If you are going to be number one you have to think and act like number one. That's what I'd done with Pepsi all along.

'Little by little I found myself irresistibly drawn to Steve's world. As Apple's lure continued to grow I felt more tension. At a Pepsi bottlers' convention I gave my first speech on personal computers, trying to convince our bottlers to use computers to manage their businesses. I borrowed heavily from my Apple meetings to show the bottlers how to use computers as a strategic tool against Coca-Cola. Then I met with Steve again, and he showed me his work on what was then a new project, the Macintosh. "This product means more to me than anything I have ever done in my whole life. I love this product and I want to share it with you. I want you to be the first person outside of Apple to see it." The nine-inch black-and-white screen lit up with some pre-released graphics. It looked to me like a miniature version of an early television set, a funny looking box. Steve then demonstrated a programme called "MacPaint". He showed me how it could draw an elaborate picture, erase it and then dump it into a trash basket on the screen.'

Taking the Plunge

'I talked to Gerry again, telling him, "There are some issues which I could never accept, and one is that there isn't enough compensation for me to give up what I have. I want a house, comparable to the home I have now. California living is more expensive as well; I don't want to worry about that." All these problems were sorted out.

'By now I had been thinking of leaving Pepsi and joining Apple for many months. Still, it was one thing to talk about leaving; it was another to physically walk out of the door. I finally left in 1985.

'I remember my last day at Pepsi, leaving with a feeling of emptiness. When I reached the downstairs lobby, I noticed that my portrait had already been taken down! I flew to my new job in Silicon Valley without packing a single suit.'

The Challenges of a New Career

'I found Apple completely different from what I had known. For 16 years at PepsiCo I had competed with the best minds in corporate

America, where power is measured by the size of one's office. At Apple, by contrast, I discovered a community without boundaries, a free-form environment, an artists' workshop. At PepsiCo we were warriors, competing fiercely over a tenth-of-a-percent of market share, and selling what Steve Jobs disdainfully called "sugared water". At Apple we are dreamers, driven by a passion to change the world, and we sell not refreshment for the body, but tools for the mind. "One person, one computer": that is our dream.

'What amazed me at first was the democratic nature of the way the business was run. There was no deference shown to the chairman. I suddenly understood what the joke quoted by Apple's advertising agency meant: "What is the difference between Apple and the boy scouts? The boy scouts have adult supervision." It was almost as if there were magnetic fields, some spiritual force mesmerizing people. Their eyes were just dazed; excitement showed on everyone's face. It was nearly a cult environment. About 100 employees had become millionaires. There wasn't a corporation in the world that wouldn't have done almost anything to get the kind of spirit and morale that people had at Apple.

'Steve and I became soul mates, speaking with each other for hours every day. At the end of each work day we would often meet for what we called a "brain dump". But Steve and I were eventually to fall apart even though he kept promising he would be better. To him, I couldn't do anything wrong. But as he became more involved in the operational side instead of just the product side things became difficult. I found it very tough trying to manage his creativity. For a long time we were the "dynamic duo", but the operational side of running Apple had always eluded Steve. At one point I remember saying, "Apple has one leader, Steve and me"; this statement proved to be a turning point.

'After the Macintosh launch I had raised Steve's title from vice-president to executive vice-president; it didn't occur to me till October 1984 that I had made a mistake. Steve and I grew apart and our relationship grew destructive. In the end I had to remove Steve from his position. I then had to manage the company out of crisis. To help me do this I picked a group of tough, irreverent managers — among them a French intellectual, a former football coach, the son of a Baptist minister, a seasoned attorney, an ex-Apple II manager and a manufacturing whiz with an English literature background — to rebuild Apple into the powerhouse that it is today.

'Apple's story is one of innovation. It's time to stop using technology simply to systematize the old ways of doing things. From its outset

Apple has offered a new view on productivity and innovation. It started with the people, not the institutions of government or business. When you think how much the personal computer has changed our world in the past decade, just imagine how far it can take us in the next. When I look back over the years I have spent at Apple I feel lucky to have been part of it all. The dream continues." '

John Sculley with John Byrne, *Odyssey: Pepsi to Apple, a Journey of Adventure, Ideas and the Future* (New York: Harper & Row, 1987), used with the kind permission of John Byrne.

Jonathan Shier:
Lawyer/
TV Executive

'My first ambition was to be a lawyer, and I studied economics and law with the intention of becoming a barrister in Melbourne in the State of Victoria. But whilst I was taking some time off and travelling around the world, I came to the UK and decided to stay here. Just for the sake of getting a job initially, I went to work for a television company, and now find I'm deputy chief executive and director of sales and marketing for Thames Television, the largest of Britain's independent TV companies. Whilst I was still in Australia, I never thought I'd end up in television, and since being in the UK, I've never thought of going back to law again.'

Background

'I decided I wanted to be a lawyer at a relatively early age, and I also knew I wanted to be a commercial lawyer, so I did economics as well as law. I then thought I ought to gain some business experience, so I finished my economics degree, joined a company, and finished my law studies part-time. I ended up in Australia's largest company — BHP, a steel and mining company — working in personnel and management development.

'I guess that during that period I decided I wanted to be a businessman rather than a lawyer. My main reason for doing that was that I've always had an international perspective. The problem with being a lawyer in Australia is that if you are admitted as a barrister in one state, you can practise in that state only. If one starts to practise as a barrister in Melbourne, Victoria, then one may well spend the rest of one's life in Melbourne, Victoria. This wasn't a great prospect for me, because I had always wanted to travel and do something different, so I decided I wanted a career that was international in scope, and one in which I wasn't tied down.

'At BHP, because it was Australia's largest company, the directors were asked by one of the Shadow Ministers in the Government to supply a young executive to work in Melbourne and Canberra as Principal Private Secretary to the Shadow Attorney-General. I was 24, vice-president of the Young Liberals, with a keen interest in politics, so I welcomed the chance when it arose. BHP, and I suspect myself, always assumed I'd be coming back to them.

'After three and a half years of writing speeches and doing research I'd reached the stage where I had to decide: either to get my own career or be an appendage to someone else all my life. When the Attorney-General died suddenly of a heart attack, I knew the time had come to move on to something different. At first I thought I might go back to being a barrister, but I wasn't sure, so I thought I'd travel the world for a couple of years.'

Considering Career Turnaround

'I visited about 150 countries while I was travelling. Then I came to London, where I met and fell in love with an English rose! I had to find a job, but I wasn't into the working-in-a-pub-in-Earl's-Court syndrome. I didn't initially have a work permit nor the right to work legally in London, so I had to go through a lot of machinations to get a job.

'The only job I thought I might do well was to work at ITN, so I thought "What do I have to do if I want to get into television?" I managed to get a very lowly job in Scottish Television. I worked there for seven years; I had to work there for five years just to satisfy my work permit. It was only during these seven years at Scottish Television that I woke up to discover that I really enjoyed working in television, and that I was reasonably good at it as well. I was then headhunted to Thames Television.'

Changes and Contrasts

'Many people I'm working with now know I was a lawyer before, they've read about my background, and my turn of phrase can be rather legalistic at times, but I wouldn't want people to think I talk like a lawyer all the time. I certainly talk like an Australian, and I guess people are more conscious of that.

'Although they're clearly two different areas of business, TV is not unlike law, in so far that they are both relatively intimidating, and you need to have a lot of self-confidence and inside knowledge. There's also a huge amount of technical and specialist *lingua franca* — buzz words — that you have to know.

'I don't miss the fact that I never went on to be a barrister — I've honestly never thought about it since I've been here in England. However, I use my lawyer's skills and training most days: selling £250,000 worth of television air-time is not so different from selling an argument in a court room or selling a policy in Parliament House; ultimately they require the same discipline. I'm a businessman first, but I love the law.

'I was brought up amongst Australia's establishment, playing cricket on the green and all that. I did find a completely different attitude in Britain in the 1970s, and I think the country's infinitely better in attitude now than it was then. It's far more entrepreneurial now, people work harder, whilst enterprise in Australia has had its problems. Australians either work hard or are very lazy. It's a wonderful lifestyle out there. The Australians who are in it for the "short haul", for deal-making, have been high-profile recently, but they're not all like that.'

The Challenges of a New Career

'You should never assume that people in television are other than "heavyweight": there are some very bright people here. It's not like going into some less-than-successful industrial business and "sorting it out". One of the big problems is management of the creatives. We do this through a combination of hugs and ruthless logic. There are shows that some may have wanted to kill off at birth, but you have to make people think again. It can be very frustrating, but I love it.

'Motivating people is 99 per cent of the job. People can be very mobile between different TV companies, and it can be quite a job to keep them, but we've cut down our turnover in marketing. The calibre of people who run media operations is quite good on the whole; the competition for those jobs is fierce.

'It's very different now, working in the highly competitive environment at Thames compared with Scottish Television, which was in more of a monopoly situation; it has been almost like another career turnaround to move from one to the other. Thames has changed a lot over the last few years, becoming much more commercial and aggressive yet more thoughtful and analytical, and perhaps less modest. We can continue to grow by producing and selling better programmes; naturally, the viewer will eventually decide which ones he or she wants to watch. This is the great challenge, helping Thames through the next few years or so.

Sandford Smith: Healthcare Executive/Biotech Company CEO

'I am currently the President and CEO of Repligen, a promising young biotech company. The majority of my business career was spent with Bristol-Myers (now Bristol-Myers Squibb), a leading pharmaceutical company. During my career, I was heavily involved in their extensive overseas operations. Along with many others, I was being considered for additional responsibility, having reached a general management position at a relatively young age. Given the stability of a large organization, it was a risky and certainly adventurous decision to take the helm of the fledgling Repligen Corporation. I believe I am a good example of an individual bitten by the biotech bug, while simultaneously attracted to the opportunity to become master of my own fate. Today we are working diligently in order to lead Repligen toward the release of its first products, which include the Repligen-Merck AIDS vaccine, AIDS therapeutics, and Platelet Factor Four, a cancer therapy agent initially to be tested in AIDS-induced Kaposi's sarcoma.'

Background

'My background is primarily in finance and gradually evolved into general management of several overseas pharmaceutical subsidiary operations. After college, I elected to work in finance and banking, starting in the International Training Program of Bank of America in San Francisco. Several years later I joined Manufacturers Hanover Trust, a New York-based bank, where eventually I became responsible for a team of officers lending to major multinational companies in the healthcare industry. This position provided me with significant exposure to the major pharmaceutical companies based in the northeast. I became so interested in the healthcare field that I decided rather than remain in banking I would switch to the corporate side and work for a healthcare organization. I was fortunate enough to join the Bristol-Myers organization, where I spent three years in international corporate finance before moving into the operations sector of their international group.

'After an apprenticeship as assistant to the president of the International Group, I was made manager of a joint venture company based in Tokyo. Thereafter, I was appointed country manager for the Bristol-Myers business in Indonesia, where I spent the next three years. After completion of this assignment and nearly five years abroad I moved back to the US Pharmaceutical and Nutritional Group as vice-president for Corporate Development and Strategic Planning. This move heralded my introduction to biotechnology, which at the time (this was 1985) was unknown to me (I had been overseas when a number of biotech companies were coming into prominence. It was then believed there would be a proliferation of recombinant DNA technology-driven products — the products of biotechnology — into the healthcare market.

'At first I was mystified by the new biologically-driven technology. "What is this all about — biologically-based products? I really do have to find out what I have missed since leaving the US" I kept saying to myself. After some preliminary investigation it became clear that biology, in combination with chemistry, would be the source of the next generation of healthcare products rather than synthetic organic chemistry by itself. How could I become more involved in the pioneering of the application of this technology?'

Considering Career Turnaround

'I began to investigate various means of direct involvement in the developing field of biotechnology. Meanwhile, my strong desire to be in a situation where I could see and shape the outcome of decisions continued to nag at me. In a billion-dollar division, time-frames are understandably long, as is the decision-making process. This can be frustrating if you are accustomed to demonstrating measurable progress in a shorter period of time, as was usually the case when I was overseas.

'Basically what led me away from a large pharmaceutical corporation and into a biotechnology career was a combination of impatience and the sense that I might be able to pioneer product development rather than just sell products developed by others. I was motivated by the concept that products would be driven by biology rather than by the more traditional synthetic chemistry avenues. I consider myself fortunate to have had a superb training and background at Bristol Myers and I will always have an enormous respect for the people with whom I worked with there for over ten years.

'The history of Repligen and how I became involved is basically quite simple. Repligen was founded in 1981 by two senior scientists from the Massachusetts Institute of Technology (MIT). They initially decided it would be productive to apply recombinant DNA techniques to the development of industrial and agricultural products. These industrious scientists established a number of research projects, attracted corporate partners, and were able to develop enough of a critical mass so that the company was able to go public in March of 1986, only five years after its founding.

'At the time Repligen went public, the research was concentrated in many diversified areas. There were projects in healthcare, personal care, pulp and paper, and agriculture. It was a very broad portfolio; too broad in fact to be practical. In 1986 the Board of Directors determined that the company needed a fresh focus. They resolved that a new leader was called for who had a certain set of skills — not necessarily a scientist, but an individual who could manage a group of scientists. That person had to be able to deal with the investors and be able to explain the new thrust of the business focus. Some financial background would also be required for this position.

'The board of directors used the services of a search firm, and in the course of that search I was identified as a candidate. After reading about Repligen and analysing the product portfolio, my first reaction was to say "Why would the Board want me at Repligen — my background is general management and marketing?" The answer was rather simple. The Board wanted an individual with proven leadership and business skills who could provide a new vision and who had the ability to make things happen.'

Taking the Plunge

'I recognized that at Repligen I would have the opportunity to hold equity in the business — something that would probably not be as material at Bristol-Myers. The flipside, or course, was that my family and I would not have the same level of security or stability. You have to make a leap of faith and think to yourself, "All right, I'm going to believe in the basic nucleus of the human resources." Once you make this leap of faith, you can't look back. After meeting with the Repligen Board, who provided their full backing, I decided that this looked like a terrific opportunity. Repligen has a group of "A" students who would not be content to muddle along with a "C" performance.

'I would agree that Americans are more willing to make this kind of leap than Europeans are. Americans are, I think, more willing to move from job to job; it's just more culturally acceptable to do this. In Europe it's still not as accepted, and in Japan it's hardly accepted at all.

'The compensation package was also important because I felt that if I was going to make the leap, the potential reward would also have to be attractive. High risk equals high reward. Today I own about 2 per cent of the outstanding stock through the mechanism of options. As the company becomes successful and the valuation rises, these options will provide substantial incentive and reward. For me, the optional payback is not only financial, it's the tremendous sense of achievement in making something happen and catalysing others to action. To build a company from scratch and make it develop provides an enormous sense of satisfaction.'

Changes and Contrasts

'I had been exposed to the biotechnology field before joining Repligen, especially in the areas of vaccines and therapeutics. At Bristol-Myers, there was simply no reason to discuss the status of internal research projects. At a major pharmaceutical company, there are more than twenty research programmes running simultaneously at any given point in time, whereas at Repligen there are only several. Because of Repligen's public and financial profile, it is necessary to discuss the status of research programmes at a much earlier point in time. Since we do not operate profitably and have no major revenue sources — investors are "betting on the outcome".

'A big company which generates profits does not have to disclose information until a product is in advanced clinical trial status. In smaller companies like Repligen, management usually speaks openly about the status product development programmes because our shareholders are essentially financing our losses, and our progress is critical to them. Progress, or the lack thereof, affects our stock price, company morale, and, of course, analytical coverage. As a CEO of a publicly-traded company, you have to keep public interest in the company at an increasing level without products on the market. You, therefore, have to keep investors and analysts current on pre-clinical and clinical developments.

'There's also another contrast with my previous role. At a major healthcare company there is only a small chance of running the whole business, of seeing the whole picture. At Bristol-Myers, I was concerned with only a small part of the whole, while at Repligen I am involved in all facets of the business. I have the opportunity to view all of our activities and play a major role in the participatory, consensus of management which we have adopted.'

The Benefit of Experience

'The experience I gained while running small business units when I was overseas with Bristol-Myers has turned out to be directly relevant to my current responsibilities. If you substitute the research organization for the sales organization, it is really quite similar. Financial management of an overseas subsidiary has also turned out to be directly applicable. While we are still burning cash at Repligen, the dynamics of financial management and expense control are basically the same in both cases. The overseas experience has been a real plus and provided excellent background in all respects except investor-related activities.

'While some of the scientifically-based managers with a highly technical background might say "No, business know-how is not so important, it is the science and technology that are most important elements of success," you have only to look at the CEOs of biotech companies today to see the real picture. The majority of them have a background in large companies, and their objectives are business-based, but must be science-driven. I think this is very important. The large company background gives you a vision of what can be achieved and the relevant hands-on experience in establishing the appropriate organizational structure.'

The Challenges of a New Career

'After management experience in a business unit of a large corporation, where the extent of your responsibility is usually finite, the prospects of taking the helm at Repligen were very exciting indeed. I joined the company at the end of 1986, about nine months after it had gone public. As I said earlier, Repligen lacked a clear focus, the scientists were demoralized, and there were several programmes that were not making scientific headway. The place really needed to be "bootstrapped", objectives established and a new game plan put into place.

'Over the course of my first year at Repligen, we accomplished two major objectives. First, we established a clear focus for the company in retrovirology and cancer research. Today, Repligen is one of the companies at the top in the field of retrovirology. As a secondary focus, we selected a new area which involves the inhibition of angiogenesis, a novel approach to the treatment of solid cell cancer. The research has progressed steadily over the last four years, and we hope our first product will enter clinical testing in early 1992. Our singular goal, which we will have to achieve in order to become successful, is the development of products that will compete in the therapeutic and vaccine sectors of the healthcare market.'

Reviewing the Situation

'In closing this interview, there is one point that I would particularly like to emphasize: the most exciting thing about biotechnology is that it's a new frontier. Those of us who have selected this field today are, in a sense, all pioneers. We are driving the application of a our technologies towards the development of products to save lives and enhance the quality of life. By applying our core technology, especially monoclonal-antibody technology and recombinant DNA technology, towards the development of new therapeutic products, we will move closer toward the ultimate goal of enhancing human life. My career turnaround hinged on the excitement of becoming a modern-day pioneer. For me, the aspect of "pioneering" a new industry was an exciting prospect and weighed heavily in my final decision.

'As a general rule, for every ten major basic research programmes, one may ultimately result in a product that enters into advanced clinical trails. To be successful at Repligen we must choose our focus very carefully, plan very carefully, spread our risks appropriately, manage our resources efficiently, provide adequate financial reserves and execute our game plan flawlessly. Science and technology must likewise co-operate fully. As in any other evolving industry which is driven by technological innovation, at the end of a day, good old-fashioned hard work, spiced with an enormous amount of luck, are the central ingredients.'

Peter Smitham: Electronics Entrepreneur/ Venture Capitalist

'After a career spent mostly in electronics, working for ITT, setting up my own electronics business and then selling it, I've found my real niche in venture capital. I've been restless and ambitious for most of my life, and I get bored easily, so I've had several career turnarounds of sorts — but leaving electronics marketing and distribution to go into venture capital has been the biggest change.'

Background

'My first job was with the Co-operative Wholesale Society. I was straight out of university and I had a lot of socialist ideas so this suited me very well. I was involved in a variety of functions with CWS — operational research, human resources and work-study exercises around different factories — and then they paid for me to go to business school, which was brilliant.

'I was involved in their management development training programme when CWS underwent a structural change in 1966. A professional managing director was appointed from the outside, and although he made many changes little happened in my area. I felt restless, found I no longer wanted to finish the programme, and left CWS. I got a job with ITT, the massive American electronics conglomerate. So my first career turnaround was leaving the grocery business for electronics, but the move was logical in so far that at CWS computers were used widely in the stock control of finished goods. And while I was not trained as an engineer, I had gained useful product rationalization skills.'

Changes and Contrasts

'The culture at ITT was amazing when I arrived there at the impressionable age of 25. We worked the most incredible hours. I put in 600 hours of unpaid overtime — they were so pleased with me that they sent me on a free holiday. I was made Managing Director, running part of ITT's Electronic Services, which employed about 200 people and dealt with selling to the engineers in the UK's major electronics firms. The business was growing rapidly into Europe, and I helped to start up and acquire businesses in Germany, France, Scandinavia and other places. It was great fun, because the electronics industry was really taking off.

'While still at ITT I was called up by a headhunter who had heard me on an Open University radio programme talking on "the use of computers." The headhunter was working for an entrepreneur who was involved in the pharmaceutical wholesale business, merging companies together, trying to achieve economies of scale and getting rid of poor quality and duplicated management. I left ITT in 1971 and worked with Tom Jermyn for two years before the business was sold out to Weston's Pharmaceuticals.

'It had been a boring business, with low margins, low costs, and very conservative and traditional relationships with chemists. In comparison ITT had been fun and radical; the pharmaceutical wholesale business there was no real concept of marketing.'

Preparing a Mission Statement

'I was thinking of joining British Leyland when a man appeared from out of my past, someone who'd been a supplier when I was at ITT. He wanted me to start an electronics distribution business and develop it, a business that would handle the same market as ITT but which would exploit their weaknesses to its own benefit. Initially I said no, although I did write out a list of what I wanted, what it would take to make me consider doing this, including the salary, the amount of equity, and how long the contract would be. The essence of the deal was that I would spend one year creating the company, then, remaining a shareholder, move on to a bigger company.

'I decided to give it a go for a year, so I set up the business (in electronic components), and attracted suppliers for whom I could sell, such as Texas Instruments, Bourns, and Union Carbide. There was a lot of competition, but I was able to convince suppliers that I could do the job and help them to increase their market share. So, at age 31, I was in my fourth "career". When the year was up I thought about returning to a large company, but the only other shareholder in my new enterprise was having problems, and if his business went bust, this would affect the financial underpinning of my company too. He said 'Come over as managing director and swap shares in one company for shares in a new holding company."

'Ten years later this business had grown dramatically — originally employing only 100 people, by 1983 there were more than 500, and the increase in turnover went from £1.3 million to £35 million. It was at that point that we sold out to Lex, who bought my shares.

'Lex had a major electronics business in the US — which was joined with their European operations. Part of the deal was that I had to sign a three-year contract agreeing to stay and run the company. Based in New York I was part of a team that ran the worldwide electronics arm of the company, with specific responsibility for Europe.

'Between 1982 and 1985 Lex enjoyed three-fold growth, from £35 million turnover to £110 million. I expanded the business organically, and I also acquired another electronics distribution company and merged it with Lex. We set up branches across Europe, with ten in Germany alone.'

Considering Career Turnaround

'Even before the Lex deal I was beginning to realize that I had been in the electronic components business for a very long time, and that I was starting to get stale. I talked to a friend who was a non-executive director of Jermyn and a lecturer at the London Business School, Stuart Timperley, and he suggested that I should take some kind of educational time off, such as a refresher course.

'I enrolled in a course at Stanford University in California, and looking back this was to have an enormous influence on my career turnaround. I joined a senior management programme of 200 executives, just for two months. There were top business people from 28 different countries, all on about $150,000. We had amongst us the Managing Director of County NatWest, the senior partner of Peat Marwick in the US, the chief executive of J. Walter Thompson in South America, and many others like them. It was at this time that I met and was impressed by venture capital people, and was attracted to their work, and discussed opportunities of working with them, although I didn't do anything about it at the time.'

Taking the Plunge

'By 1985 my contract with Lex was coming up for renewal, and I wasn't sure that I wanted to stay. Lex were very considerate but I never felt really comfortable working for them.

'I had had contact with headhunters in the past, so to help sort out what I really wanted to do, I went to see Dr John Viney in the spring of 1985. He had carried out search work for us at Lex so technically I was a client and therefore off-limits. I told him I didn't want to be involved with a big company, but he told me that my skills could be applied to either a large or small operation. We talked about which industries and types of companies would find me interesting and vice versa. He sent me to meet three other search consultants around London. Another friend of mine, who had been in a senior position in personnel at American Express, gave me a series of psychometric tests and some free counselling. He said I was a radical, good in a changing situation and with an entrepreneurial bent.'

'When my contract came up for renewal I simply resigned. This meant that I could pursue an opportunity with a venture capital firm. I joined Schroder Ventures in November 1985.

'Schroder Ventures began as a start-up by Jon Moulton, its UK managing partner. Still only 40, he's very pragmatic, a very striking personality. He saw as long ago as 1978 that leveraged buy-outs were the big business of the future. At the time, he was with Coopers & Lybrand's mergers and acquisitions group in New York, but he returned to London in 1981 with Citicorp to help to set up its new office in the UK.'

The Challenges of a New Career

'We have a portfolio of over 80 companies of most shapes and sizes, from start-ups to large buy-outs and from very high-tech to non-tech. It was Jon Moulton who introduced Schroder Ventures to the idea of employing former industrialists — such as myself — as partners to advise our clients on the decision-making involved in investment opportunities. The feature that makes us different is this management help that we can offer our clients.

'I was offered less money to join Schroder Ventures than I was making at Lex, but I didn't do it for the money. I wanted a change. Venture capital is brilliant: you can't get bored, it's so varied. Every day is so different, and you really feel you're making an impact. Running a business is 70 per cent routine, and I'm not good at that. In venture capital you can focus on the major issues. You gain an insight into industry and more importantly into what makes people tick.'

Practical Advice

'Understand yourself — what you really like and dislike. For some people it helps to talk things over with others. The real issue is if you are not happy or enjoying your job — do something about it. It amazes me that habit — going to the same company every day — gets so ingrained, and people forget to ask themselves if it's still fun. If it's not — make a change. You have to work out for yourself what it is that you want to do, and go for it. If you feel restless, you just have to keep looking until you find something you really enjoy.'